Country Roads
~ of ~
MISSOURI

A Guide Book
from Country Roads Press

Country Roads
~ of ~
MISSOURI

Archie Satterfield

Illustrated by
Clifford Winner

Country Roads Press
CASTINE • MAINE

Country Roads of Missouri
© 1994 by Archie Satterfield. All rights reserved.

Published by Country Roads Press
P.O. Box 286, Lower Main Street
Castine, Maine 04421

Text and cover design by Edith Allard.
Cover art by Victoria Sheridan.
Illustrations by Clifford Winner.
Typesetting by Camden Type 'n Graphics.

ISBN 1-56626-073-6

Library of Congress Cataloging-in-Publication Data
Satterfield, Archie.
    Country roads of Missouri / Archie Satterfield ;
illustrator, Cliff Winner.
        p.   cm.
    Includes bibliographical references and index.
    ISBN 1-56626-073-6 : $9.95
    1. Missouri—Guidebooks.   2. Automobile travel—
Missouri—Guidebooks.   I. Title.
F464.3.S28   1994
917.7804'43—dc20   94-1745
                                                        CIP

Printed in the United States of America.
10 9 8 7 6 5 4 3 2 1

To Joe Martin, of West Plains, who believed in me.

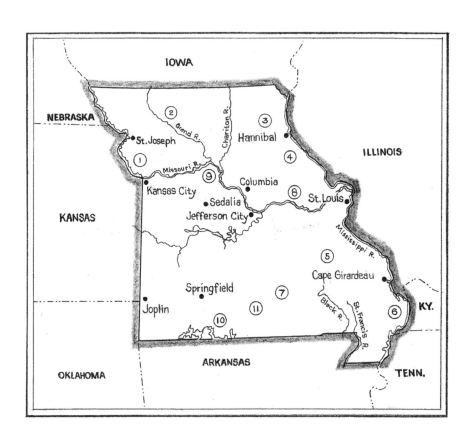

IOWA

NEBRASKA

ILLINOIS

KANSAS

OKLAHOMA

ARKANSAS

TENN.

KY.

② St.Joseph
①
Kansas City
⑨
Sedalia
Jefferson City
Columbia
③ Hannibal
④
⑧ St.Louis
⑤ Cape Girardeau
⑥
⑦
Springfield
⑪
Joplin
⑩

Grand R.
Chariton R.
Missouri R.
Mississippi R.
Black R.
St. Francis R.

Contents

(& Key to Missouri Country Roads)

Acknowledgments

Many people have been generous to me to make this home-coming book possible, and my only concern in listing them is that I will forget someone.

For my last trip I was given the use of a twenty-seven-foot Jayco Eagle motor home. Thayne Smith made the arrangements, and I am very grateful. I found it especially useful on a trip like this, because it freed me from worry about being at certain places at certain times, and I didn't have to spend two weeks packing, and then unpack every day. I could set up an office and know where all my maps and papers were, and when I stayed with friends and relatives, I could slip away early in the morning without waking the whole house. The only thing I couldn't do with the motor home was use the drive-through service at the McDonald's in Nixa, where I received the coffee I ordered but left part of the motor home's roof as a tip.

Continental Airlines, which serves both Kansas City and St. Louis, was also generous with the reduced fare they make available to travel writers. Peggy Mahoney, public relations manager, was especially helpful.

For several years Steve Kappler, public relations manager for the Missouri Division of Tourism, has been a helpful friend to writers. Steve not only is very knowledgeable about the state, he is quick to respond to requests for information and makes valuable suggestions.

In something of a catchall, blanket statement, I want to thank the many Missourians whose names I didn't get but who went out of their way to be kind to me for no other reason than I was a stranger and needed information. This includes the cabdriver in Grain Valley who, without my asking, explained that he didn't use a meter but charged by the mile and showed me the mileages he wrote on his pad. The desk clerk of the Shilo Inn at Independence allowed me to leave my luggage in the lobby while waiting for the airport shuttle, insisted I have a cup of coffee, and refused a tip when I left. I am also grateful to the woman and teenage girls who were running a book sale outside the public library in Kirksville. They charged me twenty-five cents for eight issues of the *Missouri Historical Review* and were disappointed that I didn't take the whole box at the same price.

I might not have become so interested in Missouri again had it not been for a chance meeting with an old schoolmate. My family arrived at West Plains when I was in the fifth grade, and in the class picture I am sitting beside another string-bean young gentleman named Bob Schultz. We played basketball together in high school, then went our separate ways. Nearly forty years later, he came to Seattle and we had a meal together. Bob and I have since kept in touch, and it was he who commanded me to attend our fortieth class reunion. I'll always be grateful for his persistence.

Lest you think I have been so overcome with nostalgia that I can see no wrong in Missouri, I found that there are always exceptions; two incidents I'll mention were so out of character I thought they were funny. One occurred in a small hotel. I walked in and the clerk looked up from the chair he was repairing and snapped, "Just what is it you want?" I had wanted a room, but decided I wanted out. The same thing occurred when a chain motel on I-70 tried to charge me $15 over the quoted rate for a nonsmoking room. There is only one Eden.

Acknowledgments

Some wise and honest writer once said that he stood on the shoulders of giants, meaning that his book was only as good as the other books, articles, and sundry materials he read while researching his book. Before writing this book I read several books and bought several, so I could take a bit of Missouri home with me to Seattle.

Here are some of the more useful books and articles I found:

Capper/Midwest Research Institute. *The Missouri Quick-Fact Book.* Topeka, KS: The Capper Press, 1991.

New Madrid Historical Museum. *Some Happenings of the New Madrid Earthquake 1811–1812.* Compiled by Dorothy H. Halstead.

Hubbell, Sue. "Earthquake Fever." *New Yorker*, February 11, 1991.

Ingenthron, Elmo. *Indians of the Ozark Plateau.* Branson, MO: The Ozarks Mountaineer, 1970–1983.

———. *Borderland Rebellion.* Branson, MO: The Ozarks Mountaineer, 1980.

Bittersweet, Inc. *Bittersweet Country.* Edited by Ellen Gray Massey. Garden City, NY: Anchor Press, 1978.

In the Heart of Ozark Mountain Country. Edited by Frank Reuter. Reeds Spring, MO: White Oak Publishing, 1993.

And finally, I must give credit to the book *Roads & Their Builders,* published by the Missouri State Highway Commission, if for no other reason than the pleasure in reading this statement by one Isaac van Bibber, Jr., while trying to promote travel along the Boonslick Road in about 1865:

Who will join in the march to the Rocky Mountains with me? A sort of high-pressure, double-cylinder, go-it-ahead, forty-wild-cats-tearin' sort of feller? Wake up, ye sleepy heads . . . Git out of this brick kiln . . .

these mortality turners and murder mills, where they render all the lard out of a feller until he is too lean to sweat. Git out of this warming-pan, ye hollyhocks, and go out to the West where you may be seen.

Now that's enthusiasm.

Introduction

The research for this book was a reintroduction to the state of my birth, and it was a wonderful experience. Just think: I was paid to go back and see things I hadn't seen in many years, to see places I had never seen, to look up friends from high school. The last trip was in October: the weather was clear and cool, and the floods of 1993 had stopped temporarily. I didn't dare complain about working conditions.

It is so true that you have to leave a place or lose a thing to realize the value of what you had. Missouri is a place I left in my youth and I seldom returned. It wasn't exactly a divorce from my place of birth when I left in 1959 and moved to Seattle, but it was close. After spending four years in the navy, I decided I wanted to live the rest of my life near saltwater. Also on my wish list was a place where I could see mountains high enough to keep snow all year, and having a moderate climate without high humidity or tornadoes or ice storms. I have always been afraid of snakes, and that was factored into my search for a home. I got almost everything on my list when I moved to Seattle.

It took more than two decades for me to rediscover the wonderful things I left behind. In truth, this book is the result of several trips to Missouri over the past four to five years: to visit relatives and friends; to attend a funeral; to attend the fortieth reunion of my high school class in West Plains; to write stories about the Ozarks and the Missouri wine industry, and finally to make the trip to research this book.

When I left Missouri in 1959, the Ozarks where I grew up were still a very poor place. In recent years life has improved for nearly everyone, and the modest homes—those are waffle words for shacks—are difficult to find. The one I saw most recently had been unoccupied for several years but was still standing. It had belonged to one of my uncles and his large family, and was covered with pseudobrick siding, had a tin roof (which made rain- and hailstorms memorable), and was wallpapered with newspapers. It had just four rooms—the living room, two bedrooms, and a kitchen that doubled as a bathroom once a week when water was heated on the woodstove and poured into the tub placed behind the stove for privacy. That kitchen stove was the sole source of heat for the house. When I stayed overnight I remember standing in front of the stove wrapped in a blanket, or perhaps a handmade quilt, until I was warm, then racing off to the straw pallet in the corner of the living room and going to sleep before the cold set in. A porch ran across the front of the house; I believe it once had wire screening around it, but no trace of the screen remained.

My hometown of West Plains, where my parents moved so we could have a good education, is almost exactly halfway between Springfield and Poplar Bluff, each 100 miles away. I was always impressed when someone said that they had to go over to Springfield. It was really cause for comment if they went there and back in the same day. During my last trip to Missouri I drove more than 500 miles—*in a single day!* As my late mother would have said while contemplating the unbelievable, "Well, I'll be."

Missouri seemed so large then. I am reminded of a film made during the late 1950s about Mark Twain. In one scene he went back to his boyhood home in Hannibal and commented on how much smaller his room was than he remembered. When my father went away to work in northern Missouri and Iowa during an occasional summer to bring home some cash, it seemed he was going to the edge of the earth. Yet in 1993 I drove from Eudora, Kansas, to the Iowa border, then over to the Mississippi River, with several stops—all in a single day.

Now I know how the Oregon Trail veteran Ezra Meeker must have felt. During his long and colorful life he went from St. Joseph to the Pacific Ocean in a wagon train, then years later went by wagon all the way back to Washington, D.C., then home again the same way. Next he rode a train over the trail, then traversed it in an automobile. Before he died he flew over the Oregon Trail in an airplane. Ezra makes my adventures sound puny indeed.

With the exception of a week or two every October, I had never thought of Missouri as a particularly pretty place. It always surprised me when people talked about its beauty. All I remembered was the hard work of hauling rocks out of the fields, chopping sprouts (Missourians' term for newly sprouted trees), hoeing in my mother's large garden, and being either too hot in August or too cold in January. I always dreaded the first few weeks of school in September because the temperatures were still at summer level and no school I knew had air-conditioning.

The coldest temperature I ever experienced was one January morning in West Plains when it dropped to −28 degrees Fahrenheit. Oddly, that was the year I quit school to go to a ranch in Colorado. I had just returned home because it got too cold for me out west: −22 degrees.

Armed with these memories, it took me a while to warm up to Missouri. I suppose it began when I went back to visit my son, who was attending Washington University in St. Louis. I returned again to visit a lovely woman. I timed that visit with when I thought the best fall colors would be displayed, then found that it had been a wet summer and the colors were either too late or too bland. I returned to Seattle with nearly all the film I had bought, still in its wrappers, unexposed. The plus side of that trip was that I had never seen southeast Missouri, and I had a wonderful time traveling around the area from Cape Girardeau south to New Madrid and along the Mississippi River. On the way down I saw the Bollinger Mill and the Sandy Creek Covered Bridge. One Sunday I drove over to the Wappapelo area to see something I didn't know Missouri had—swamps.

On another trip I had an assignment to write a story about the Hermann-Washington area along the Missouri River with an emphasis on the wine industry. This was one of my favorite trips, because I stayed in one of the old homes that had been converted to a bed and breakfast, went to a party at another bed and breakfast, saw Hermann when very few people were there, and had lunch with a high school friend.

On yet another trip I drove through Hermann and found it so filled with people for a festival that policemen were conducting traffic. I like to write about interesting towns, but I don't care to participate in the festivals we travel writers help encourage, so I didn't stop.

The research for this book also showed me the great diversity in Missouri, and the sad and fascinating Civil War history and its importance in the settling of the West. Missouri was the launching pad for the Oregon Trail, the Mormon Trail, the Santa Fe Trail, and the Lewis and Clark Trail (although Illinois might argue with this, since the explorers camped near Alton to keep their men out of trouble in St. Louis before they crossed the Mississippi to start up the Missouri River). Missouri is where the Pony Express started, and the Missouri River was the equivalent of the interstate highway system for trappers and traders.

One of the most pleasant surprises was the excellent highway system without the annoying tollbooths so prevalent in Kansas and Oklahoma. All through Missouri you'll find well-maintained two-lane blacktop highways—so many, in fact, that I seldom drove on gravel roads. To my surprise, the roads into Howards Ridge, where I was born in Ozark County, are paved now.

Plotting a research trip for one of these guides is like those puzzles where you are supposed to connect a series of dots with one continuous line. I was never good at those puzzles, and it probably shows on these pages. But I tried. In an attempt to give the book some kind of direction, I have written it roughly in the order I traveled the state on my last two visits: I followed one large circular route with other trips scattered in between. When I couldn't make the lines connect, I improvised.

Part of the fun of traveling country roads is bumbling along and stopping at country stores, flea markets, and yard sales, taking wrong turns and having to backtrack, buying a bottle of pop from a human being rather than a machine, and eating where locals eat. The best breakfast I had in Missouri was at the Stockyard Cafe in Nixa: sausage, biscuits and gravy, and good conversation about round bales of hay and the price of cattle. Because Nixa is close to the Arkansas line, I also heard the latest President and Mrs. Clinton jokes.

If you are traveling in Missouri with no real destination, find one of these gathering places and ask what you should see or do in the area. This way you will find an interesting old building, a beauty spot that hasn't been made into a park yet, a genuine country store, or the best farm auction you've ever seen. Of course you may also see the new high school track, and the town's new street signs, and be asked to comment on the new paint job on the hardware store. Once I asked a man in southeastern Missouri what the people around there were most proud of. Even though it was about ten o'clock at night, he drove me across town to look at a tree I could hardly see that had been struck by lightning. No matter. Moments like this make you momentarily part of the community.

This is the kind of traveling a small boy or a happy dog might do. You never quite know where you're going next and you never travel in a straight line. Most important, you always have time to look at new things.

No book could possibly cover all the interesting places I saw while doing this research. Although you may think the book is a little heavy on the Civil War, think how much I left out. The same applies to all the Ozark folklore I could have included.

Many, many roads deserve to be in the book, including some that I drove en route to those selected. One of the prettiest drives was from Nixa to Ava on State 14. I left Nixa early on a foggy morning in a motor home and was continually frustrated because I couldn't find places to park so I could take photographs of the sun coming through the fog and trees. When I was in high school we lived near the junction of State 14 and US 63, and I would like to have included the highway, but I settled for driving on it as part of the route to see gristmills. Perhaps I can write about the route—Ava and the Trappist Monastery, Twin Bridges, and Siloam Springs—in the next edition of this book.

I had a wonderful time exploring Missouri and kept finding new bits of information that fascinated me, especially related to the Civil War, which I didn't know had been fought in so many places in the state. History is one of my greatest interests; I am eternally fascinated by the paintings of Thomas Hart and George Caleb Bingham, and I can't cross the Missouri River without wanting to sing "Oh Shenandoah."

But to travel without human contact is sight-seeing, not a lot different than watching a slide show or a television program. Although I remember the wonderful scenery and the historic buildings and the foggy mornings with the sun coming through the fog and oak trees, the things I remember most are my contacts with people. I remember the two women I happened upon who were fishing in the Mississippi River a few miles south of the town of Louisiana. I remember the people I talked to at flea markets and service stations, and the elderly woman in the hardware store in Gainesville who took the time to help me look for something she was certain she didn't have, telling me, "but there's so much junk in here you never know what you're going to find." That could be my credo as a traveler: you may think you know what to expect from a place, but be prepared for something else.

To simplify road designations, I've used the following abbreviations: I = interstate, US = U.S. route or highway, State = state route or highway, and County = secondary state, provincial, and county highways.

1 ~

Kansas

City to

Weston and

St. Joseph

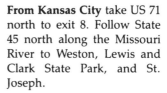

From **Kansas City** take US 71 north to exit 8. Follow State 45 north along the Missouri River to Weston, Lewis and Clark State Park, and St. Joseph.

Highlights: *Missouri River bottomlands, picturesque small towns, the historic town of Weston, Lewis and Clark State Park, and historic St. Joseph.*

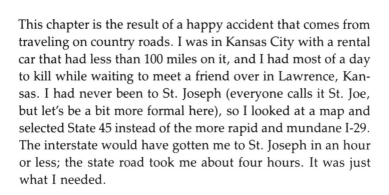

This chapter is the result of a happy accident that comes from traveling on country roads. I was in Kansas City with a rental car that had less than 100 miles on it, and I had most of a day to kill while waiting to meet a friend over in Lawrence, Kansas. I had never been to St. Joseph (everyone calls it St. Joe, but let's be a bit more formal here), so I looked at a map and selected State 45 instead of the more rapid and mundane I-29. The interstate would have gotten me to St. Joseph in an hour or less; the state road took me about four hours. It was just what I needed.

The drive was so pretty that if I had not been expected in Lawrence that afternoon, I would have spent five or six hours on the trip. The primary reason for the drive—to see St. Joseph—was almost abandoned in favor of Weston, a small town off the highway built on a series of steep hills overlooking a flat area where the Missouri River once ran.

The first surprise after leaving Kansas City was the size of the Missouri River. Since it is one of the most famous rivers in America and was the trappers' and traders' route west, and I have seen it thousands of times, in my mind it is always a large, broad river. Although I doubt that I could throw a coin across it, the Missouri above Kansas City is proof that size doesn't always play a role in importance.

Much of the route north from Kansas City is through hilly country. The highway runs along the inland edge of the river bottomland rather than cutting across the middle, where it would waste good farmland and also be subject to flooding. It was along this highway—State 45—that I first began making notes, describing the road as a "double-yellow-line highway," an accurate description of rural highways in hilly country.

Although much of the bottomland is still farmed, many of the homes built on the low hillsides look suburban, and I assumed they were owned by people who work in Kansas City and commute daily. Most of the hills are thick with oak, which gives them an almost fluffy look in the haze that so often blankets Missouri. In October the hills become a patchwork quilt with spots of different colors in the dense woods.

Although I should have known how thick the woods were from my childhood in the Ozarks, where we had to chop oak, sumac, and many other kinds of sprouts, I was curious, so I pulled over for a closer look at the timber. Sure enough, it was too thick to walk through without tearing my clothes. I could see the ground, now being covered with a new layer of autumn leaves, but the sprouts, saplings, and mature trees grew as thick as a full beard.

Some very small towns are scattered along the river; one of the prettiest is Farley, with a population of 217. Farley is a sensible town because it was built on a hill high enough to escape the floods and to make the town, with its distinctive brick church, more picturesque than if it had been built on the flats. Besides, I am a grouch in my belief that farmland should be used for crops, not parking lots. It seems to me that we should not cover even an acre of farmland, but instead should put our homes, businesses, churches, factories, and supermarkets on land that can't be cultivated. Many years ago when I worked for a small newspaper, I computed how many acres of land is taken out of production by a mile of freeway. The story was not popular with the state and federal highway folks.

The high point of this trip is Weston, roughly halfway between Kansas City and St. Joseph on State 45. Weston was platted in 1837 on a series of steep hills overlooking the Missouri River and was settled by southerners, followed by a scattering of Germans, Austrians, and Swiss. It soon became one of Missouri's most important river towns because of its location just above where the Missouri takes a right turn to the north. For a while Weston was the second largest port in the state, behind St. Louis.

The first farmers in the area raised hemp and tobacco. Today Weston is the only place in Missouri that still raises tobacco; in the fall you'll see bunches of the big leaves hanging in barns to dry. Steamboats landed here regularly, and the town had a brewery and two flour mills. The McCormick Distillery, still in operation, was founded in 1856. By the time the Civil War broke out, Weston had a population of around 5,000 and was an important stop on the Oregon Trail. Almost

3

as many wagon trains heading west crossed the Missouri at Weston as up north at St. Joseph.

Then the town was hit by a series of disasters. Most of the downtown area was destroyed in two major fires early in its history, and this was followed by five floods. The last left the river channel about two miles away, where it has stayed ever since. The population of Weston dwindled to around 1,000 by 1890.

Here it stayed for ninety years, until the Weston Development Company (WDC) was formed to breathe new life into the town. An inventory of the town's advantages included more than 100 residences dating before the Civil War and the largest number of antebellum homes in the state. The WDC worked with community organizations to have the downtown area designated a historic district and placed on the National Register of Historic Places. This occurred in 1972, and the restoration of the downtown area continues.

Weston has antique and collectible shops galore, art galleries, at least four bed and breakfasts, the McCormick Distillery, Mission Creek and Pritle's Weston wineries, an orchard with a retail outlet, three museums, and special events throughout the year.

Five miles north of Weston on State 45, you'll find hills being used for other than building homes with views and raising oak timber. The Snow Creek Ski Area is one of the few ski areas in the state, and it has two triple chairlifts, nine intermediate trails, and three rope tows in the beginner area. It is open for night skiing and also has snowmaking equipment.

State 45 north straightens out after leaving Weston, and by the time it reaches Lewis and Clark State Park and joins US 59, the sense of being on a country road is beginning to dissipate. The park covers 120 acres on the shore of Sugar Lake and has camping, boating, fishing, and swimming.

This is one of hundreds of places along the Missouri honoring the explorers Captains Meriwether Lewis and William Clark. It is doubtful that any of the western pioneers had more places named in their honor than these two dedicated men.

Just after the United States bought the Louisiana Purchase from France in 1803, President Thomas Jefferson appointed Capt. Meriwether Lewis to lead an expedition to the Pacific Ocean and bring back volumes of reports so that the government would know whether to try and obtain the remaining land between the two oceans. Nobody really knew what was out there, and the search for the Northwest Passage from the East Coast to the West Coast was still very much a subject of speculation. Explorers knew of the mighty Columbia River, but they didn't know what lay between it and the Missouri. Jefferson wondered if the Missouri might complete the route between the oceans. He hoped that it was simply a matter of crossing a low divide between the two river systems.

This concern with the whole continent was part of the Manifest Destiny doctrine making the rounds in America, a justification for taking land that didn't necessarily belong to the United States. In staking a claim across the whole continent, the United States had to deal not only with the French (who had now sold their claim to the U.S.) but also with the Spanish, who had vague claims on the desert and the Pacific Coast; the English, who then had most of Canada and were elbowing their way down to meet the Spanish; and the Russians, who had Alaska and were in and out of the Hawaiian Islands and the Pacific Northwest coast down to California.

The Lewis and Clark expedition was clearly a major undertaking. Although an army officer was leading it, Jefferson did not want it to be a military venture. It was to be an exploration only; go in as quietly as possible, meet with local governments and tell them about the change in ownership, see what was there, and come home with complete reports on virtually everything—zoology, anthropology, botany, politics, geography, cartography, celestial movements, ethnography, and so on. Jefferson let Lewis select his own crew; Lewis immediately chose as his co-commander an old friend, Lt. William Clark. Lewis told Clark that nobody should know that their ranks weren't equal, and that they would both be known as captains. Lewis began his trip in Washington, then went up to Pittsburgh to start assembling his crew and to buy a boat. They floated down the Ohio River to the Mississippi, with an occasional stop to take on more men. When the boat entered the Mississippi, the crew had to paddle and tow the boat up the river to a camp in the St. Louis vicinity. The captains decided to put themselves some distance from the temptations of St. Louis and camped across the river; they spent the winter of 1803–4 trying to turn a group of independent woodsmen into a unit.

In addition to the experienced woodsmen they hired, Lewis and Clark also took on a military detachment to escort the party up the Missouri River to their winter quarters and help them with the enormous amount of food, clothing, and scientific equipment they had to carry.

During that summer of 1804 they rowed and towed their boats upstream and made note of many places still recognizable today: caves they camped in, streams entering the Missouri, and prominent landmarks. They were into the Dakotas by fall, and they built a small fortress, named it Fort Mandan, and wintered over.

Come spring, these extra men floated back down the Missouri to St. Louis, leaving Lewis and Clark and their party of twenty-eight men, one woman (Sacajawea), and one child (she gave birth to a son that winter). The explorers struck out into the unknown when ice cleared from the Missouri. They spent the spring, summer, and fall of 1805 going up the Missouri almost to its headwaters, bought horses from Sacajawea's relatives, then crossed a low pass into what is now Idaho. They almost starved to death in the Bitterroot Range before they staggered into the Nez Perce villages along the Clearwater River. They ate fish that probably didn't agree with their weakened bodies, and many fell ill. When they had enough canoes purchased or built, they launched them in the Snake River, some men still too weak to do anything other than lie in the canoes and hope. They survived the terrible rapids of the Snake, entered the Columbia, and got safely through the rapids and waterfalls of the Columbia Gorge. They arrived at the mouth of the Columbia River in November 1805.

They spent the winter of 1805–6 at Fort Clatsop, which they built near present-day Astoria, Oregon, and left for home in the spring of 1806. They paddled up the Columbia and the Snake and retraced their path back into Montana. There they split into two parties; Clark's group went south to catch the Yellowstone River and followed it down to its confluence with the Missouri, near what is now the Montana–North Dakota state line. Lewis led the group going north into the Blackfoot country on the Marias and Milk Rivers. They got into a running fight with a Blackfoot band, and the group almost killed their horses on the ride back to the Missouri. They made the rest of the downriver trip with Captain Lewis lying prone on the floor of a raft, a musket ball in his buttocks. It was put there by a crewman named Pierre Cruzatte, who was blind in one eye and weak-sighted in the other. Cruzatte had mistaken Lewis for a deer.

The two captains have been heroes to me since I first read about them, if for no other reason than they got their orders from President Thomas Jefferson—among the most detailed orders in American history—and they followed the orders exactly. When you study the history of the expedition and realize how difficult the trip was, you have no choice but to be impressed with the dedication of these men. They worked very hard for more than two years under extreme conditions, and never once complained that too much was expected of them or that they had a stomachache or that they simply weren't in the mood to write that day.

They treated the Indians with courtesy, but the tribes must have been a little curious about these men who told them they had a new Great White Father when they didn't know they had one at all. But to the explorers' credit, they never treated the Indians as childlike savages or cannon fodder. They were under orders from Jefferson not to get involved in battles with them. They did only once, when Blackfeet tried to ambush them.

This doesn't mean that Lewis and Clark were doormats for the Indians. To the contrary: on the explorers' return trip up the Columbia and Snake Rivers, an Indian ridiculed them for eating dog meat; the natives' diet of fish and camas roots was giving the men the "back door trots." Clark almost came to blows with the ridiculer, and did in fact fling a puppy at him. Message delivered, message received. The Indian backed off.

Clark was probably a bit easier to take than the serious, perhaps unstable Lewis, who tended to be a bit of a prude. Clark seemed to enjoy the personalities of his companions and the Indians they met along the way, accepting them as they were. Clark had a sense of humor, which showed from time to time in the journals, and which he couldn't always contain. When describing the social skills of the Clatsop Indians, which were sorely lacking by Washington, D.C., standards, Clark gleefully described their gastronomical and bathroom habits.

Along their route from Wood River near Alton, Illinois, to Astoria, Oregon, you'll see special highway markers com-

The Pony Express Museum in St. Joseph

memorating their trip. Most of their campsites have been identified, all along the Missouri River to its headwaters in Montana, the Clearwater, Snake and Columbia Rivers, plus side trips they took in Montana.

How well did they do their work? According to the great Lewis and Clark scholar Paul Russell Cutright, they accomplished these things: they initiated the first official relations between the United States and Native Americans along the route from Missouri to the Columbia watershed; they discovered the Shoshoni, Flathead, Nez Perce, Yakima, Walula, and Wishram tribes; and they did the first language studies in at least six new linguistic groups.

In addition, they ended the long search for the fabled Northwest Passage. They established that the North American

9

continent was much wider than previously believed—many thought it ended just beyond the Rocky Mountains—with the discovery that two mountain systems separated the Missouri headwaters from the Pacific. They discovered and thoroughly described at least 170 plants new to botanists and at least 120 new birds and animals.

As a footnote to history, since Lewis started at Washington, D.C., this trip made him the first American on record to travel overland from the Atlantic to the Pacific.

After passing the Lewis and Clark State Park, the remaining twenty miles into St. Joseph are beside a railroad track, across a bridge that spans Contrary Creek, and between farms some distance from the Missouri River. Almost suddenly the highway enters St. Joseph, one of Missouri's most historical towns and worth a leisurely visit. This was an important transportation point during the 1800s, and many people heading west to the Pacific Coast came to St. Joseph overland along the Missouri River and across the top of the state; others arrived by steamboat from St. Louis.

The pony express stables have been preserved to tell the story of the pony express, which began on April 3, 1860, and ended a few months later when the first intercontinental telegraph line was completed. Jesse James figures prominently in the area. Next door to the Patee House, the first headquarters of the pony express, is the house in which James was killed in 1882.

In the Area

Weston Development Company (Weston):
816-386-2909

Snow Creek Ski Area (Weston): 816-386-2200

Lewis and Clark State Park (Weston):
816-579-5564

St. Joseph Area Chamber of Commerce (St. Joseph):
816-232-4461

Pritle's Weston Vineyards (Weston): 816-386-5588

McCormick Distilling Company (Weston):
816-386-2276

2 ~

Gallatin,

Jamesport,

and

Kirksville

Take State 6 from St. Joseph, on the Kansas border, east to Kirksville.

Highlights: *Gallatin and its rich history, the Amish community around Jamesport, rolling hills, and pretty small towns.*

Before starting this circular trip around Missouri, I checked with a few friends and inquired in bookstores—but to no avail—for basic information on the state. When I arrived in Kirksville I went to a store on the square called Books and Things, and they not only had a copy of *The Missouri Quick-Fact Book*, they also gave me a senior-citizen discount.

Unfortunately I had already driven most of this route without knowing what to expect in advance. I didn't even go through Gallatin—the highway loops around it—because I didn't know about its historical events.

State 6 begins in downtown St. Joseph as an extension of Frederick Boulevard, ducks under US 71, and heads east across farmland. It bumps against US 36 and ricochets due north for about ten miles, then goes back to its east-northeast direction across the dark farmlands of northern Missouri. It was this rich soil that incited jealousy in those of us who grew up on the rocky, sandy soil of the Ozark Highlands.

It was early October when I drove through this area. Front porches and windows were already filled with pumpkins, and goblins dressed in overalls lounged on porch swings and were draped over mailboxes in anticipation of Halloween. Laundry hung from some clotheslines, and for a fleeting moment I remembered how much better sheets and pillowcases smell when they have been dried in the wind.

It was also on State 6 that I first noticed one of the major forms of recreation for country folk that is also a way to generate income while cleaning house and meeting new people: it's that great American event known as a garage sale. It seems that every fourth or fifth house along the country highways has a sign and a few tables with what some call junktiques—old electrical appliances, curtain rods, bottles and jars, picture frames, magazine racks, automotive accessories, and so forth. In many towns these garage sales become flea markets on the main drag or out by the main intersection.

They are addictive. I wanted a few items to put in a motor home I would be using in a few days, and I became obsessed with finding a plain old stove-top coffee percolator, the kind you put on the stove and wait for it to percolate, then judge the flavor of the bubbling coffee by its color. I stopped at a farmhouse outside Gallatin, and I stopped at a community garage sale down near Thayer. I parked precariously on a narrow shoulder near Kirksville, and just outside Mexico I had a nice chat with an elderly man about the local football team. I could have saved time by going to a hardware store,

13

but the thrill of the chase overpowered my good sense. I knew that only the gregarious at heart have garage sales, so my search was always a good way to kick-start a conversation. When I packed up to fly home, no stove-top percolator was in my luggage. But I met some friendly people through my mild little adventures.

As I said before, the highway goes around the northern edge of Gallatin. I can't remember why I didn't stop, but I should have. Only after I bought the fact book in Kirksville did I discover that Gallatin is famous in the history of the Old West for the 1883 trial of Frank James for the murder of William Westfall, a train conductor, and Frank McMillan, a passenger, during a robbery two years earlier.

Frank James was acquitted; he was about the only member of the James and Younger gang to have a normal life after the others died. Jesse was killed by Robert Ford in his home in St. Joseph. Jesse had gathered a group to plan another robbery, and just after breakfast Jesse got up from the table to straighten a picture on the wall and Ford shot him in the back. Ford became a hated hero and later was murdered himself. In one of those ironies of life, after Frank's acquittal he helped support himself by going on the lecture circuit to preach that crime doesn't pay; of course, he was standing up there making his crimes pay very handsomely.

A short distance north of Gallatin is a religious shrine that is sacred to Mormons because it was here that the Mormons stopped after being driven out of a series of towns. While Joseph Smith, the founder, was here with his followers, he announced that this spot, named Adam-Ondi-Ahman, was where Adam offered sacrifices to God after he and Eve had been driven from the Garden of Eden.

As I drove east from Gallatin, I soon found myself in Amish country. The first clue was beautifully tended farmhouses and barns, with no electrical power or telephone lines

Amish boy plowing outside Jamesport

leading in from the lines along the highway. The next clue wasn't so subtle. I began meeting and passing the distinctive enclosed black buggies pulled by one horse and decorated with a vivid international orange triangle on the back to alert drivers. The third clue came at the edge of town and had nothing to do with the Amish. A "Welcome to Jamesport" sign hung from the side of an ancient combine beside the road.

The Amish came to the Jamesport area from Ohio and Pennsylvania in the 1950s during one of their periodic migrations when their present communities become too crowded. A local resident noted that some members of the Jamesport community have recently begun moving south to the Carrollton and Windsor areas.

The most noticeable aspect of the Amish religion is that they do not believe in modern conveniences such as electricity and telephones, and they make their own clothing. Their religion does not permit photographs of themselves, so the local chamber of commerce makes a point of telling visitors that they should not photograph the Amish.

The religious order began in Switzerland when a group led by Jacob Ammann broke away from the Mennonites. The Amish believe in separation from the world and do not go to war, swear oaths, or hold public office. They hold religious meetings in homes and they limit education to the eighth grade.

The Amish presence has helped make Jamesport one of Missouri's most rural-looking towns. The black buggies share the streets with motor vehicles, and when I drove through, two Amish men were loading sacks of feed into their large wagons drawn by a team of horses. A flea market stretched along the main street for almost a block. At last count the town with a population of less than 600 had sixteen antique shops, twenty-six specialty shops (selling quilts, dolls, rugs, crafts, and so on), and two companies that specialize in tours of the Amish community. I was told that a short distance south of town are two stores owned by the Amish, one a bulk-food store and the other specializing in the fabrics they prefer for clothing, linen, curtains, and other uses.

The identity brought by the Amish has helped keep the town from fading away entirely. Before 1925 it had a population of more than 5,000 and was the busiest railroad town between Chicago and Kansas City; an average of forty trains went through daily. It was also the largest shipping port in Missouri. Now it is a combination farm town and tourist destination. Several festivals are held there throughout the year, and guided tours take visitors through the town and out into the countryside to call on Amish families.

Jamesport is also the hometown of America's most-produced children's playwright. Aurand Harris wrote *Punch and Judy* and the musical adaptation of *Androcles and the Lion*, among many other plays.

After leaving Jamesport, State 6 heads northeast along the hills and valleys into Trenton, another of those neatly arranged towns you come to expect in areas with good farmland. The town has a population of about 6,000 and has lots of brick houses; there is also a distinctive courthouse with a tall steeple, and other equally impressive public buildings. In spite of having many buildings made of brick, but because of the impressive public buildings, Trenton bears a slightly European look.

The Thompson River, a fair-size stream, flows through the edge of town, but it isn't long before you cross No Creek. That's its name. I thought about stopping to ask how it was named, but I was afraid the answer wouldn't be as interesting as the speculation. Did its name mean there wasn't a creek there at all—just a dry bed? Maybe somebody said no to somebody beside the creek. Or does it represent denial of some dastardly deed? It is one of my life's minor mysteries.

From Trenton the highway winds its way through more and more timber—oak and pine with thickets of blackberries and sumac. The towns are small but well tended, except for an occasional church needing a coat of paint, which for all I know means that the congregation has shifted its allegiance to another church. Things like that happen.

After Galt, Humphrey, and Reger, and hundreds of acres of hay fields dotted with round bales, Milan appears. This is the Sullivan County seat, a pretty town of about 1,700 with several old, comfortable homes and an unhurried look about it.

Next comes Green City, a crossroads town with the Richard Widmark Airport. Richard Widmark? Isn't he from the East Coast? It turned out that the actor once was a partner in a cattle feedlot in Green City, and when he came to check on his investment, he landed his plane at the local airport. The airport needed a longer runway, so Widmark donated enough land to make the extension possible. The locals showed their gratitude by naming the airport for him.

The timber becomes thicker as you drive on eastward, and many fencerows are marked with trees as well as posts and wire. The last town before Kirksville is Novinger, which has about 500 residents now but once was a major coal-mining area. The Coal Miners Museum tells this part of its history, and the Isaac and Samuel Novinger Log Home is a two-story home built about 1848 that has been restored by a local organization.

With a population of about 18,000, Kirksville is the major town in this part of Missouri. It has Northeast Missouri State University and a totally unpretentious and friendly downtown district around an old-fashioned square. Its downtown buildings are old but not worn out, and when you ask someone for directions, they stop what they are doing, look you in the eye, and take their time with the directions to be sure you understand them. I like that. It reminds me of New Zealand. When you ask directions there, people stop what they're doing and take you where you want to go, then insist you come over for dinner that night. Northern Missouri isn't quite that friendly, but you'll get help when you need it.

In the Area

Jamesport Community Association (Jamesport):
816-684-6146

St. Joseph Area Chamber of Commerce (St. Joseph):
816-232-4461 (for information on Gallatin)

Gallatin, Jamesport, and Kirksville

Trenton Area Chamber of Commerce (Trenton):
816-359-4324

Kirksville Area Chamber of Commerce (Kirksville):
816-665-3766

Coal Miners Museum (Novinger): 816-488-5174

Isaac and Samuel Novinger Log Home (Novinger):
816-488-5280

3 ~

Of

Christian

Communes

and Covered

Bridges

From the Iowa state line near the northeast corner of Missouri, take State 15 south through Memphis, Edina, Novelty, Bethel, Paris, and on to Mexico.

Highlights: *Bethel with its unique Oregon Trail story; Paris with its many historical buildings, including the birthplace of Mark Twain, and the Union Covered Bridge.*

My reason for taking State 15 south from Edina was to see two towns that are off the main route. They are Novelty and Cherry Box. In my typical blundering fashion, I glanced at the map without really studying it and headed south on State 15; before long I was caught in a big traffic jam caused by the Harvest Fest in the small town of Bethel.

When I finally found a place to pull over south of Bethel, I looked more closely at the map and saw that Novelty was west of my route. It and Cherry Box are still struggling along without making my acquaintance. Irritated with myself, I tossed the map in the cardboard box that served as my on-the-road filing cabinet and kept going south.

The festival in Bethel had attracted thousands of people, and the streets on the parade route were lined with people sitting in folding chairs, standing patiently, sitting on the grass, walking around in search of someone or a place to sit. It was something of a shock after driving through the quiet countryside with so little traffic, but I knew something about this town of only about 100 residents from a previous visit and from my readings of Pacific Northwest history.

Bethel is one of the most thoroughly studied towns in the state. It compares well with Hermann as a cornerstone of the German immigrants' experience in Missouri, but Bethel is a clear winner in the eccentric sweepstakes.

Bethel was founded in 1845 by a Prussian immigrant named Wilhelm Keil, who with his wife, Louise, came to America in 1835, the same year some religious leaders in both Europe and America predicted that Christ would return to earth. The Keils lived in New York for a while, then Pennsylvania, then Ohio. Keil was a charismatic man; after he had been in America awhile, he became an ordained preacher, then left organized religion to start his own brand of Christian communism. He sometimes led people to believe he was the Messiah; detractors didn't say he exactly told them he was the Messiah, but he never denied it when asked. It seems that bold men such as Keil can always find people so disappointed with their lives that they will without question follow someone who looks them in the eye and tells them they'll take good care of them.

Keil's followers were not stupid people. When he organized his Society of Bethel, the commune became enormously wealthy. Not only did the members do well as farmers with communal crops and livestock, they also built a glove factory, a whiskey distillery, a wagon shop, and a tool factory. They built the best plows in that part of Missouri. They settled in northeast Missouri on the banks of the North River, which flows east into the Mississippi some forty miles away. They named their town Bethel, then they spread out in the area and established the nearby towns of Hebron, Elim, Mamri, and Nineveh, north of Kirksville, which was later changed to Connelsville.

The colony had done so well that by the time the great migration to the Oregon Country began, Keil wanted to spread his community and its teachings to this new land. This is what led to one of the strangest stories from the American frontier. Keil had sent some members of his group to the Oregon Country with a wagon train to search for a likely place. They came back a year or so later with the recommendation that the colony be established on the broad and beautiful—but perpetually damp—land bordering Willapa Bay, just north of the Columbia River. They reasoned that the stormy and deadly Columbia River bar was more of a barrier than an avenue of trade, and that Willapa Bay, with its protected waters, would become the major port and that railroads and highways would transport goods around the mouth of the Columbia.

Thus armed with information and a destination, Keil decided to lead the group of pilgrims himself, and he left his son, August, in charge of the Bethel colony. The strong genes of the father did not pass down to this son, however, and although residents were said to be personally fond of August, in later years they noted that he was often drunk.

Keil set the spring of 1855 as the departure date. Perhaps it was partly because that date would be exactly twenty years after his arrival in the United States and exactly ten years after he led the establishment of the communities in Missouri headquartered in Bethel.

Another son, Wilhelm, Jr., or Willie, was appointed to go along with his father, and he was excited about the prospect.

Then the nineteen-year-old youth fell ill with malaria, one of the most dreaded diseases of the period. Malaria was one of the prime reasons that families and communities left the Midwest and Southeast for the Oregon Country.

When young Willie fell ill, everyone assumed he would die long before the departure date of May 23, 1855. He did, but during his brief illness when he was lucid, he pleaded with his father to take him along. When he became delirious from the fever, he imagined himself leading the wagon train across the prairies and the mountains to that cool, green, clean land at the edge of the continent. His father promised Willie he would, indeed, go with them, and before the boy died Keil ordered that a special wagon be built for Willie. It carried a tank into which the boy's body was placed; then the tank was filled with alcohol to preserve the body until their arrival at their new home on Willapa Bay.

From Bethel to Willapa Bay, legend and fact become intermingled, but the story of Dr. Wilhelm Keil is already so off center that we might as well believe everything that has been written. The best version is that Willie did lead the wagon train across the continent because Keil ordered the hearse to be the lead wagon all the way. The best version also states that the Indians along the way heard of the hearse leading a wagon train and were afraid of it, and that when a band of Indians who hadn't heard of the strange procession drove away several head of the Bethelites' cattle, other Indians who knew the story forced the thieves to return the cattle.

This makes for good reading, and it could well be true. At least the basic facts are correct. The Bethel wagon train consisted of thirty-five wagons and about 175 people. It has been written that the Bethelites were the most wealthy group to cross the plains. When the wagon train reached Willapa Bay, one of the first tasks was to give Willie a decent burial. A site was chosen a short distance inland on a knoll overlooking the

A covered wagon at Bethel

Willapa River not far from where it enters the bay. There the grave remains today, protected by Washington's smallest state park.

The trip across the country fed Dr. Keil's messianic opinion of himself, and he sent epistles back to his followers. An excerpt from one letter follows:

> The whole desert cried out that we should perish here
> . . .There was nothing for us to do but proceed from
> sunrise to the setting sun, and curst this region of hell
> and death. I gave orders that no wagon should be left
> behind, and declared that I meant to take my people

through the desert even if all the seven princes of darkness should oppose us. I did get all our people and wagons through and the devil was put to shame. We met hundreds of Indians at Salmon Falls who were glad to see my face. I had power over the Indians and could do with them whatever I wanted to do.

Keil and his group weren't impressed with the town site on Willapa Bay after all. They knew it would not be a good place for their business interests, and they were right. Willapa Bay never developed as a port, except as a place to ship logs to the Orient. The bay has no large towns, and the major commerce around it is timber, oyster farming, cranberries, and tourism.

After looking around the Northwest at some length, Keil settled on a town site south of Portland overlooking the Willamette River. He named this settlement Aurora for his daughter, who would die in 1864 of smallpox. He and his group remained in Aurora until Keil died.

Over the next dozen years, other groups of Bethelites migrated to the Oregon Country: forty-two wagons in 1863, eleven in 1865, fifteen in 1867. Others came by ship around Cape Horn until more than 600 came out from Missouri. The dream of Christian communism died with Keil, and two years after his death the community divided everything into personal property and went about their lives much as their neighbors. The same thing happened in Bethel.

Many of Bethel's original homes and public buildings still stand, including the post office, the community hall where bachelors had to sleep, the bandstand, and some store buildings. One of the five hand-dug wells is still used. The entire town is a National Historic Site, and is the host to numerous special events throughout the year, including the Harvest Fest in October. A few years earlier I was there in July and had lunch in Colony Fest Hall. Rooms were rented upstairs, but when I saw the sagging beds and the absence of air-conditioning, I quickly decided that nostalgia and historical accuracy have their place, but not in my life unless absolutely essential. I drove over to the Mississippi and followed it south to a motel with air-conditioning.

The drive south from Bethel is through more rolling hills and rich farmland, and lots of timber spotted here and there in draws, on a few hilltops, and along fencerows. The fields had tons and tons of rolled hay instead of the bales I knew intimately as a teenager. It doesn't take you long to learn that you will share the highways and roads with farm equipment: combines, tractors, and assorted machines. Some move along at a fast clip but not in the fifty-five-mile-per-hour range, so be prepared for occasional slowdowns and be patient.

Also be prepared for one driving characteristic I notice more in the Midwest than anywhere else I've driven. When people prepare to turn off the highway, they almost come to a complete stop before doing so. I'm accustomed to people slowing and turning, but with some rapidity. Most midwesterners I watched drove as though they had a dozen eggs rolling around in the seat beside them, and I almost rear-ended one or two before I caught on to their method: flick on turn signal, slow to crawl, turn slowly, then resume speed. Once when I came home from the navy in the early 1950s, I borrowed my brother's car for a trip in the Ozarks. He warned me of another midwestern trait: farmers who drive trucks and pull farm machinery behind tractors swing wide when they prepare to make a right turn, crossing over into the left lane. Force of habit. They do it even when driving a Honda. True, not all people in rural areas drive this way, but I found enough to force me to keep up my guard.

The next town is Paris, which has several points of interest even though it is listed as having fewer than 2,000 residents. It is the birthplace of Samuel L. Clemens, better known as Mark Twain. The two-room cabin in which Missouri's most famous writer was born is now a museum. A short distance away is Mark Twain State Park.

Paris also has a Norman Rockwell connection: the artist came to Paris and painted a series on the theme of a country editor. He used the office and employees of the *Monroe County Appeal* as models for the series.

Nine miles southwest of Paris (take State 24 west five miles, then County C west one-quarter mile) is the Union Covered Bridge, which was built in 1871 across the Elk Fork of the Salt River. The bridge is 125 feet long and $17^{1}/_{2}$ feet wide. It was built for $5,000 and is still in good shape. However, it is virtually impossible to photograph because brush has grown up around it. My photos from the side reveal an unidentifiable white slab of something in the trees. Photographing the bridge head-on is equally unsatisfying because it could be a barn door or a façade. There. I feel better for getting that grumble out of my system, but I hope the caretakers of the bridge do something about that brush for other photographers.

To get back to the main road, take County AA east and watch for signs aiming you down a narrow road that leads back to State 15.

This route ends in Mexico, a bustling town of about 12,000. It is known for its American Saddle Horse, a breed popular in the area. The Audrain Historical and American Saddle Horse Museum displays artifacts relating to the breed. At one time Mexico was the major fire-clay manufacturing place in America. Almost every brick used in Missouri for buildings and streets came from Mexico, thanks to an enormous deposit of clay found beneath the town.

From Mexico you can continue south on US 54 to the Missouri River, or do as I did and drive east to the Mississippi to explore State 79, which runs from Hannibal to St. Louis.

In the Area

Bethel German Colony (Bethel): 314-284-6493

Mark Twain Lake & Cannon Dam Area Development
Association (Perry): 314-565-2228

Mexico Area Chamber of Commerce (Mexico):
314-581-2765

4 ~

Along the Great River Road

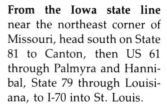

From the Iowa state line near the northeast corner of Missouri, head south on State 81 to Canton, then US 61 through Palmyra and Hannibal, State 79 through Louisiana, to I-70 into St. Louis.

Highlights: *The Mississippi River and barge traffic, the Mark Twain town of Hannibal, Louisiana and its beautiful homes and park overlooking the Mississippi, old towns and villages along the river.*

Although this route begins on the Iowa state line and goes through several towns before disappearing in the traffic of St. Louis, this stretch of the Mississippi River is dominated by one man and the many characters and events he wrote about. The man was Samuel Langhorne Clemens, alias Mark Twain (1835–1910). This entire corner of the state is referred to as Mark Twain Country. It is doubtful that anyone else who ever lived in Missouri was as universally loved, although it took a few Hannibal citizens a while to forgive him for a few things he said.

29

This route begins in the very northeast corner of the state. I didn't know until now that the Mississippi isn't the only river that forms Missouri's eastern boundary. For approximately twenty miles the Des Moines River cuts off Missouri's northeast corner that normally would have gone straight on to the Mississippi. Here at this jagged boundary, State 81 comes down from Iowa.

Only a few miles into Missouri, on the banks of the Des Moines River, is the Battle of Athens State Park. At this 390-acre site, the northernmost Civil War battle west of the Mississippi was fought in 1861. Here the Union troops defeated the Missouri State Guard. One prominent reminder of the battle is the Benning House, nicknamed the Cannonball House because you can still see where the cannonballs hit it.

Kahoka, the first town on State 81, is the seat of Clark County and has about 2,000 residents. The local historical museum has kept the beam from which Bill Young was hung after his acquittal of mass-murder charges. More pleasant memories come from the Bluegrass Festival each August, and the Mule Festival in September.

About halfway between Kahoka and Canton is the very small town of St. Patrick, which has the distinction of being the only town in America named for the Irish saint. A chapel has been built in the town to commemorate the man credited, among other things, with making Ireland snake-free.

Canton is a river town of about 2,000 near one of the many dams and locks built along the Mississippi. Canton is also known for its Remember When Toy Museum, which has more than 10,000 antique toys on display.

US 24 and 61 combine for four lanes south to Hannibal. There's something so forceful about four-lane highways that I can't help myself: I shut down all my systems except what is required to keep my foot on the accelerator and the nose of the car pointed in the right direction. So when this highway came between me and Hannibal, I spent as little time on it as possible without stopping in La Grange or Palmyra. I wanted to see old Sam Clemens's area.

Clemens wasn't a big man, but his alter ego, Mark Twain, casts a shadow across Missouri as long as that of Harry S. Truman. For most Americans, and millions elsewhere, Mark Twain and the Mississippi River are so tightly intermingled that without him the river would be big and muddy, and not much else. It certainly wouldn't hold that romance for people all over the world, and we wouldn't be so likely to look at it and dream of floating down it on a raft.

Mark Twain is the best thing that ever happened to Hannibal. Without him it would be no more famous than its neighboring town to the south, Louisiana, or Keokuk, Illinois, to the north. There aren't that many towns in America so closely identified with a citizen. John Steinbeck and Monterey, California, Thomas Wolfe and Asheville, North Carolina, and only a few others come to mind. But I don't think any are as strong as Twain and Hannibal.

Not only is Twain important to Hannibal, he is also generally credited with creating the American novel with *The Adventures of Tom Sawyer*. In spite of the dark undertones of it and its companion novel, *The Adventures of Huckleberry Finn*, Twain is also considered America's greatest humorist.

(By the way, does everyone know by now that Clemens took the name Mark Twain because he heard those words so often while he worked on riverboats on the Mississippi, and that it means two fathoms, or twelve feet?)

Hannibal works its relationship with Twain as much as it can, and it is a major industry for the town. An average of 250,000 people visit Hannibal each year. Virtually every event throughout the year is somehow tied to Twain and the characters in his books. There is a Huck Finn Shopping Center west of town and Mark Twain Lake farther west of town. Cardiff

Riverboat at Hannibal

Hill was so named because Twain once said it reminded him of hills in Cardiff, Wales. The part of US 36 that goes through town is called Mark Twain Avenue. There's an Injun Joe Campground, the Mark Twain Outdoor Theater, and the Mark Twain Cave and Campground. There's Sawyer's Creek Fun Park and Christmas Shop, the riverboat *Mark Twain*, a tour named Twainland Express with a pseudolocomotive, and a horse-drawn wagon ride called the Mark Twain Clopper. There's a shop named Aunt Polly's Handcrafts and a restaurant named Huck's Homestead.

Each Fourth of July is the end of the weeklong National Tom Sawyer Days that feature a national fence painting contest, a jumping frog contest, Tomboy Sawyer contests, and pie-eating contests. There's also a mud volleyball game; the year I was there on the Fourth of July, hotels had signs at the door to keep out these particular athletes.

The house Twain grew up in, which is two blocks up the hill from the town's gigantic grain elevators, was recently restored. It has exhibits that include a lock of Twain's hair, and photos from his life and of people on whom he based his characters. His mother became Aunt Polly, Laura Hawkins became Becky Thatcher, and Tom Blankenship was Huck Finn. Upstairs is Tom's room, with the window he climbed out to meet Huck.

Adjoining the home is the Mark Twain Museum, with many mementos, including rare first editions of his numerous books, one of his white suits, some of his favorite pipes, and one of his desks.

Next door is Becky Thatcher's (Laura Hawkins's) house, which has been turned into a bookstore below with two rooms upstairs with period decorations.

Another Clemens home is the 1830 Pilaster House, in which the Clemens family lived for about a year when the senior Clemens, an attorney, became so debt-ridden that they had to move out of their home. A statue of Tom and Huck is at the foot of Cardiff Hill and on the crest is the lighthouse built in 1935 to honor Twain.

No doubt the town has many more Twain connections, in names of shops, businesses, confections, gifts, and articles of clothing. It all seems to work for everyone. On my first visit many years ago while going to school at the University of Missouri, I was beginning to feel overwhelmed by the whole thing and started muttering that we should leave and find a real town. My companion, an English literature professor at Stevens College, put it all back into a manageable perspective: "If Mark Twain walked down the street today, he'd hurt himself laughing."

The river route continues south from Hannibal on State 79, an honest-to-goodness country highway with only two lanes, lots of double yellow lines, blind curves, modest farmhouses, blackberry vines in fencerows, and thickets you just know are sheltering coveys of quail. Off to the left, never far away, is the great Mississippi River. Sometimes you can see it through the trees, which means that you'll see much more of it—and the river traffic—in winter when the trees are stripped of leaves.

The old stern-wheelers and paddle wheelers with their steam engines and whistles have their own charm, but I am more interested in the barges and towboats that work the Mississippi. These boats are built for the task at hand and not for looks, and they are enormously powerful. They push barges strung together for what looks like a quarter of a mile, so heavily loaded they seem to be sinking. I can't stand on the bank and watch this barge traffic without feeling I could as well be watching a science-fiction film about the adventures of the men who operate commercial spacecraft.

The first town south of Hannibal on State 79 is Louisiana, one of the most beautiful on the route. It is a stately town built on the bluffs high above the river. The town has won at least one award for having such a well-maintained collection of Victorian business buildings. It has mansions on the bluff overlooking the US 54 bridge that crosses the river. A small park amid the mansions affords great views, as does the park down at river level with a high stone wall and steps leading to the water.

Although Louisiana doesn't do a lot to promote itself as a tourist destination, it recently hung beautiful banners through the downtown district with a historic homes theme, and at least three of its old mansions have been turned into bed and breakfasts.

About ten miles downriver on State 79 is Clarksville, also built along the steep bluffs but not so high that it entirely escaped the floods of 1992–93. Clarksville has a skyride to a high hill nearby, and several bed and breakfasts. The last of the locks and dams on the river, prosaically named Lock and Dam No. 24, has a viewing platform; the lake behind the dam created habitat for the bald eagles that frequent the area. As a result, each winter the town hosts Eagle Days, with the cooperation of the Missouri Department of Conservation.

State 79 continues its two-lane, winding ways along the river, usually sticking to the bluffs but occasionally dropping down into the bottomland. The road goes through towns such as Annada, which has grain elevators beside the railroad track, and Elsberry, which has a large nursery with ornamental trees on hills beside the highway. Winfield, which has a ferry over to Illinois, is a junky and funky little town beside the highway.

From Winfield, the traffic increases; the highway moves away from the river and is soon gobbled up by I-70 at O'Fallon.

In the Area

Battle of Athens State Park (Revere): 314-877-3871

Remember When Toy Museum (Canton): 314-288-3995

Hannibal Visitors & Convention Bureau (Hannibal): 314-221-2477

Louisiana Chamber of Commerce (Louisiana): 314-754-5921

5 ~

From St. Louis to Cape Girardeau

From St. Louis take State 21 south from Gravois Avenue to State 34, then proceed east to State 72 and on to Cape Girardeau.

Highlights: *Covered bridges, a gristmill, the highest point in Missouri, the lead-mining district, and unusual rock formations in state parks.*

This route begins in the heart of St. Louis on Gravois Avenue, one of those streets I remember from my childhood. My sisters lived in St. Louis when I was growing up, and occasionally I spent a week with one or the other. When I was quite young I liked staying with the married one because she had two children who weren't a lot younger than I was. When I reached my teens, I preferred living with the one who was still single, because she shared a large apartment with three women in their early twenties. I liked that a lot.

Gravois Avenue was a street I heard streetcar conductors calling out, along with Kingshighway, Chippewa (one called it Chippewa-chippy), Chouteau, Hodiamont, Chain of Rocks Road, Natural Bridge, and so forth. All are names that represent the old St. Louis to me, the St. Louis of Stan Musial, Marty Marion, and Enos Slaughter.

When I decided to take this trip down State 21, I made a point of starting as far down Gravois as I could, which was an exit off I-55 just south of I-44. Then I drove out into St. Louis County and swung south on State 21, went under US 61 and I-255, and soon was in the suburbs. They began thinning out, and before long they left me on a good country highway with hills and curves and small towns.

My first stop was the Sandy Creek Covered Bridge, a short distance off the highway. It wasn't in use but had been well cared for and had a new coat of bright red paint, which made it reflect brightly in the creek.

After leaving the bridge, towns are few and farms and barns many. This is broken country with steep but low hills, outcroppings of rocks, and lots of timber. State 21 is a popular route for St. Louis *Post-Dispatch* photographers, who come out in October for the autumn foliage photos the whole world loves. Occasionally you will come to a stretch of highway with the trees from each side touching each other as they form a canopy overhead. I went for a walk in a grove of oak trees that surrounded a roadside park and discovered that walking on autumn leaves is about as noisy as walking on potato chips. No sneaking up on unsuspecting game in these conditions.

Not far off the highway about fourteen miles north of Potosi is Washington State Park. Its 1,415 acres were once ceremonial grounds for Native Americans. The park was created in part to protect a collection of petroglyphs you can see.

South of Potosi the route climbs to the crest of the hills and goes through Missouri's main lead-mining district, believed to be the richest in the world. The mines are expected to eventually yield more than 17 million tons of lead valued at

Covered bridge at Sandy Creek

more than $5 billion. Most of the mines are in the Viburnum Trend district, in the area between State 21 and State 19 in Mark Twain National Forest.

The highway was having a lawn-ornament population explosion when I drove through. It seemed that every front yard had a zoo of miniature deer (never life-size because they might be used for target practice in—or out—of hunting season), ducks, squirrels, geese, and all manner of other small birds and beasts.

This area has two other places worth stopping for a look. The first is Elephant Rocks State Park near Belleview. Gigantic red granite rocks are rounded and bear some resemblance to a chain of elephants marching trunk to tail. The rocks are more than a billion years old, according to geologists. The park has Missouri's first self-guiding Braille trail, and is also popular with the elderly because the trails have gentle grades. No camping is allowed at the park, but there are several shaded picnic sites.

The other stop is off the highway just south of Ironton on County CC, which leads to the top of Taum Sauk Mountain. This is the highest point in Missouri, 1,772 feet. Nearby is a state park with an unusual name: Johnson's Shut-Ins State Park. It got its name from the small canyons of gorges, called shut-ins, created by the Black River. The 2,500-acre park will be one of the major trailheads for the Ozark Trail that will run 500 miles through Missouri and Arkansas.

About ten miles northwest of State 21 is the Taum Sauk Pumped Storage Plant, one of the few hydroelectric projects anywhere to recycle its water. A 55-acre reservoir was built on Profitt Mountain, with a tunnel leading down to the power plant, where the water turns turbines before going into a 400-acre lake below the powerhouse. At night when power demands are low, the water is pumped back to the Profitt Mountain pool to be used again the next day. It is a concept that I wish power companies would use in the West instead of damming all water that moves.

Ironton, a picturesque town of about 1,500, is in the heart of Arcadia Valley. Not far east of town is the Fort Davidson

State Historic Site, with some earthworks remaining of the Civil War battlefield where the Battle of Pilot Knob was fought. The battle lasted only a few minutes, but more than 1,200 soldiers were wounded or killed, most of whom were Confederates. This battle stopped the Confederate drive toward St. Louis.

All across the state I had been aware of how clean the roadsides are, and knew it was because I had been seeing signs from the Adopt-a-Highway Program, which is taken more seriously in Missouri than in most states. When this book was being written, more than 3,000 individual stretches of highway had been adopted by a business or some other organization, and the numbers continue to rise.

The program is relatively simple. A company, a church, a fraternity or sorority, a service club, high school organizations, or any other group volunteers to pick up litter from a stretch of highway at least two miles long from two to six times a year. These highways aren't only the high-profile interstates and U.S. highways. You'll see the Adopt-a-Highway signs on all kinds of roads, and on most of the roads described in this book.

The program started in Texas in 1985 when a district engineer named James R. Evans came up with the idea as a means of cleaning up litter and making people aware of it. His idea was a win-win proposal. The state highway department got the help it needed, the public became aware of littering, and an organization got a useful project and publicity from the signs.

The program's growth in Missouri was beyond anyone's highest expectations. In June 1986, there were 300 groups. A year later there were 2,300. In 1993 there were more than 3,000.

After this program was so successful, the state then embarked on two more programs. One was to encourage citizens to help mow grass along the highways, and the other encourages people to plant flowers, wildflowers, and native grasses along the highways.

You can follow State 21 to State 49 just south of Ironton, then follow State 49 to State 34. Head east, crossing US 67, toward Cape Girardeau, but plan on one more important stop—the Bollinger Mill State Historic Site.

I arrived late in the day and was the only person walking around the area. The sun was low and hit the front of the mill and the side of the covered bridge. Water in the small holding pool was dark and flowed quietly over the dam. It is one of the prettiest historic spots in the state. The mill stands four stories tall and is made of brick. The Burfordville Covered Bridge right next to the mill is one of only four remaining in the state (Union, Dillard, and Sandy Creek are the others). The bridge was started in 1858, but the Civil War halted construction until 1868.

Guided tours of the mill are offered daily during the summer months. Photographers prefer the morning light because it hits the mill and bridge at better angles than in the evening.

It is only a short drive to I-55 and Cape Girardeau, so I was tempted to add a little interest to my trip by taking a brief detour so I could touch four states in a very short time. Missouri is bordered by more states than any other in the country—Iowa, Nebraska, Kansas, Oklahoma, Arkansas, Illinois, Kentucky, and Tennessee—and I have never been in Kentucky or Tennessee. By crossing the Mississippi at Cape Girardeau, I could touch on Illinois, Kentucky, and Tennessee without driving much farther. But my sense of integrity prevailed. I do not believe in visiting a place just to add another notch to my list of countries or states visited or mountains climbed or anything else. I insist on my lists being the result of more real reasons, so those states will have to wait.

41

In the Area

Washington State Park (DeSoto): 314-586-2995

Elephant Rocks State Park (Belleview): 314-697-5395

Johnson's Shut-Ins State Park (Middlebrook):
314-546-2450

Bollinger Mill State Historic Site (Burfordville):
314-243-4591

Adopt-a-Highway Program (Jefferson City): 314-751-2551
(Information is also available from any district office.)

6 ~

Earthquake
Country

From I-55 south of Sikeston, in southeast Missouri, take State 80 east and State 77 south to Towosahgy State Historic Site. Then head west on County MM and County YY to State 102. Follow it south to Big Oak Tree State Park. Continue south on State 102 to County WW and head west to New Madrid. For a loop trip, return to Sikeston on I-55.

Highlights: *A once-fortified Indian village with several earthen mounds intact, and a grove of the tallest oak trees in America. The loop ends at New Madrid, epicenter of North America's strongest earthquake.*

Although this eastern bulge in Missouri is less than 100 miles from where I grew up, it seemed so far away that it could have been somewhere east of West Virginia. I remember Ozarkians talking about the bottomland over toward the Mississippi and they claimed not to like it. They said they'd rather chop sprouts and pick up rocks than chop cotton beneath the summer sun, but I think they were envious of the rich soil and the large checks farmers picked up at the end of the season.

I was more than fifty years old before I saw this part of the state, and I drove into it on a zigging and zagging route south from St. Louis to be sure I saw the Sandy Creek Covered

Bridge and the Bollinger Mill and Burfordville Covered Bridge on the way. Even in my middle years I wasn't prepared for how different it is from the Ozarks. Undoubtedly hills exist in this area that some call "swampeast," but all I remember is mile upon mile of flat black land with white puffs of cotton. Being accustomed to hills, mountains, coastlines, and other natural boundaries, I was glad when my friend drove me over to Dorena so we could sit on the bank of the Mississippi and watch a ferry cross over from Hickman, Kentucky.

This area—only a short distance down the Mississippi from where the Ohio enters—is one of the most interesting areas along the entire river. Here the river has formed a peninsula of sorts, so that Missouri protrudes over into Illinois and Kentucky before turning southwest and returning to almost the same longitude as Cape Girardeau. This large peninsula contains three places of interest to anthropologists, botanists, and geologists, and all three sites are very close together and can be visited easily in a day.

Towosahgy State Historic Site is a sixty-four-acre tract that contains one of the best-preserved Osage Indian villages. Its name means "Old Town" in the Osage language; carbon dating shows that the town was inhabited for about 400 years, beginning about the year 1000.

Unlike many of their relatives who roamed over much of Missouri, these Osage were urban folk and didn't leave the area except perhaps to trade. The town was protected by a fortification wall of timber that surrounded the earthen mounds they built. The village had six of these mounds, the largest of which was 250 feet long and 180 feet wide and stood about 16 feet high. Wooden structures were built on them and plastered over with clay and mud.

These mounds were common throughout much of the middle Mississippi Valley. The largest and best known is the Cahokia Mounds, directly across the Mississippi from St. Louis near East St. Louis. The purpose of the mounds isn't known exactly, but archaeologists working in the area once conducted an experiment and used students and volunteers as a labor pool, having them construct a mound using tools similar to those of the Mound Builders. They found that the mounds would be built in a surprisingly short time.

The Towosahgy site has produced some surprises to archaeologists digging there. In 1970 they found remains of a tower, or bastion, and determined that more probably existed around the stockade. They found evidence that the inhabitants dug down several inches for their floors, and that garbage pits were dug beside each house site. In them was evidence of their diet of corn, beans, persimmons, wild plums, and deer. Not much else is known of these people because the site had been abandoned more than a century before the first Europeans came to the area, and the first archaeologists didn't begin arriving until toward the end of the nineteenth century.

It is a pity that more isn't known about this group of Osage, because the Osage were one of the more interesting nations of Native Americans. In general, they were a well-organized nation with an economy based on hunting, gathering, and farming. They planted crops of corn, beans, pumpkins, and squash in the spring, then took off for the summer months on hunting expeditions without bothering to fence or guard their crops. They dried much of the meat they killed, and when they returned in the late summer, they harvested the crops and hung part of this food to dry, too. In the fall they gathered nuts and wild fruits.

The Osage were noted for their height; most men were six feet or more tall. Nearly every European who encountered them was impressed with their appearance and their air of confidence. The Osage didn't think much of the Europeans, because these men who lived on the fringe of society often had matted and filthy hair, wore stinking clothing, and were in general disgusting to these people who took cleanliness so seriously that they plucked much of their body hair. They were so obsessed with body size and appearance that they tried several methods of making their children tall. One was to flatten the back of babies' heads so that the head would be an inch or two taller than normal.

Before we give the Osage Noble Savage status, it is wise to remember that although they were good to look at, they were still people, no better or worse than any other group of people on earth. The Osage were slave traders long before the Europeans imported Africans. They frequently raided other tribes to capture new slaves to use in their own bands or to sell to other tribes. They sometimes married the women they captured and reared the children. They became full-scale middlemen after the arrival of the Europeans, and captured Indian slaves for the French slave market that operated at the mouth of the Arkansas River.

The Osage had an unusual approach to marriage, and it was closely tied to their concept of manhood. When a family selected a young warrior to marry a daughter, a four-day wedding was the result—a very formal, stylized function involving tattooing and various religious symbols. Once the marriage was consummated, the warrior then inherited all the bride's sisters, who also became his wives so that he could spread his valuable seeds among several rather than only one. In this way the Osage practiced selective breeding to ensure that the characteristics they liked would be perpetuated.

This practice had a cruel downside. With one man taking care of several women, the other young men who had not passed the rigid tests leading to manhood were forced to spend their lives without wives. They became what the

Europeans called "squawmen"; they were forced to dress like women, they did the work of women, and they were required to live a life of celibacy so that their weak genes would not be passed along to the next generation.

The Osage were one of the many tribes taken to reservations in Kansas and Oklahoma. Not understanding the concept of land ownership or exactly how they could be uprooted from their traditional land, the Osage tribe sold its Kansas holdings and was left with no land to call their own. Ironically, the Osage were among the Oklahoma Indians who became wealthy when oil was discovered on their land. Today they live on in Missouri through some geographic names they left behind, the Towosahgy site, and a scattering of other reminders of their presence.

Only a short drive on State 102, Big Oak Tree State Park covers 1,000 acres to protect one of the few remaining stands of virgin timber. The rest was leveled during the pioneer years of agriculture when levees were built to drain the swamps for farming and logging. This started about the turn of the nineteenth century. When the New Madrid earthquakes hit in 1811, millions of acres along the river sank as much as fifty feet, creating even more swampland that would soon kill the forests. The reclamation went on for more than a hundred years, and by 1930 most of the swamps were gone. Then came the loggers and sawmills, then came the plows. Soon most of the trees were gone, replaced by crops.

The stand of trees in this state park survived the ax and saw. Even though the Great Depression had most of America on its economic knees, local businessmen took up the cause to protect this last stand of timber, and schoolchildren donated pennies, nickels, and dimes to the cause. In 1938 just over 1,000 acres were purchased and the Big Oak Tree State Park came into being.

Big Oak Tree State Park

Among the towering oak, elm, and hickory trees stand a dozen trees that are the tallest of their species in Missouri, and two that are the tallest in America. In addition to these trees, the park has green ash, swamp cottonwood, American elm, black willow, persimmon, silver maple, bald cypress, and giant cane. There is also poison ivy and stinging nettles, but you don't have to worry about them because a boardwalk keeps you at a safe distance while keeping your feet dry.

Bird-watchers also like the park because 146 species of birds have been counted there, including some that are rare to Missouri—the hooded warbler, the Mississippi kite, and Swainson's warbler.

County WW takes you west from the park to the small town of New Madrid (MAD-rid), site of the strongest earthquake ever recorded in North America, and perhaps in the world. The immense area covered, and the catastrophic changes the earthquakes brought, have led some seismologists to believe that the New Madrid shocks had a magnitude of XII on the Mercalli intensity scale of I to XII. This scale, which used Roman numerals, was the forefather of the Richter scale (developed in 1938). XII meant total destruction; the San Francisco earthquake of 1906 was rated only as a VII.

Whatever the exact intensity, and there's no way of knowing, there can be little doubt of its severity, because enough people lived in the area to give consistent and equally terrifying accounts.

New Madrid was one of the first areas in Missouri to be settled. Two Canadian trappers, François and Joseph LeSieur, established a trading post there in 1783 for a St. Louis merchant named Gabriel Cerre. They called the region L'Anse à la Graisse (Cove of Grease, because buffalo and bear, sources of grease, were in the area). But in 1789 George Morgan, a veteran of the Revolutionary War, came in and laid out a large city and called it New Madrid in hopes that the Spanish would look favorably on his undertaking. Morgan didn't stay around long, but the Spanish built a fort and collected duties on the river traffic. By the end of the eighteenth century an estimated 600 persons lived in the area.

The first quake hit at about 2 A.M. on December 8, 1811, and caused the earth to rise and fall like waves in the ocean. The earth waves continued throughout that day and for several more days, gradually diminishing. Another strong shock came on December 16 and continued all through that day and the next. The shocks continued for several more days, again diminishing in strength; then on January 23, 1812, another shock hit that residents said was as strong as the first. Still another strong one hit on February 7, which was to be the last big one. It wasn't over, though; nearly every day for nearly two years residents felt the earth move, sometimes gently and other times not so gently.

A man in Louisville and another in Ste. Genevieve set out to count all the tremors, but both gave up when they numbered in the hundreds. Researchers have since estimated more than 1,900 separate tremors strong enough to be felt 200 miles away.

The result was catastrophic beyond imagination. The Mississippi was dammed at one point and flowed backward. A waterfall was created upstream from New Madrid, then was swept away. The course of the river changed several times, and riverbanks were swept into the current. Trees and parts of houses and barns were swept back and forth as the earth waves created havoc on the river. Islands disappeared and new ones were created. Lakes beside the river were drained and new ones created.

Large areas of the earth fell up to fifteen feet, including the original town of New Madrid, which disappeared forever. Vast fissures were created, then closed, expelling tons of water, sand, and charcoal into the air. Often the air was filled with the stench of sulfur and rotting vegetation. One man told of falling into one of these fissures and of seeing occasional flashes of light, apparently from gases being ignited. The sounds of the earthquakes must have been terrifying: the explosions in the fissures, the creaking and groaning of the tortured earth, the roar of the river, and the new waterfalls.

The direction of the river was changed forever. In Kentucky, Reelfoot Lake was created when the river rushed in to fill one of the many depressions created when the earth dropped. The lake, now part of a wildlife refuge, is about fourteen miles long, five miles wide, and an average of eighteen feet deep, which is the depth that this part of the earth fell. Immediately after the earthquakes, the lake was more than 100 miles long.

New Madrid was relatively quiet after the earthquakes finally ended. But during the Civil War it was the scene of an odd battle. The Confederate forces had been building fortifications along the Mississippi River, and when they lost Forts Donelson and Henry in Kentucky, they moved downstream and set up a stronghold at New Madrid and on No. 10 Island, which was the tenth island downstream from the Ohio. The Union soldiers marched in from Sikeston; the Confederates tried to stop the Union army's advance by sending out a few men carrying guidons to make it look as though they were many. The Union didn't bite, and instead attacked; the Confederate general barely escaped back inside his compound with the Union riders on his heels. The Union bombardment of the Confederates continued from the night of March 12 through the day and into the night of March 13.

During the night of March 13 the Confederates held a council and realized that their situation was hopeless. When morning came on the fourteenth, the Union officers prepared to launch an attack, and all men were at their battle stations waiting for the order. Suddenly two faint forms emerged from the thick fog. They were Confederates carrying white flags. They explained that the area had been abandoned during the night and they had slept through the retreat.

As an aside, historians tell us that 1,162 military actions occurred in Missouri during the Civil War.

New Madrid got a lot of attention, and some frazzled nerves, in 1990 when a persuasive man named Iben Browning said that there was a one-in-two chance that another devastating earthquake would hit the New Madrid area about December 3, 1990. Although most people doubted him—he was not a trained seismologist, and what scientific training he had was largely self-taught—still there was enough publicity surrounding his prediction that New Madrid was host to news crews from all over the United States. It was one of those situations where the news industry was damned if they did send a crew to cover it because it was stupid, and damned if they didn't because the prediction just might be accurate.

Missouri writer Sue Hubbell counted more than fifty vehicles with news logos and satellite dishes before "like Dr. Robertson, who had counted the tremors of 1811–12, I got tired and quit. I looked local, so I was interviewed a lot." Although many people were understandably nervous about the proceedings, there were enough unusual occurrences to keep people telling stories for years to come. One radio station brought along a 350-pound man and had him jump up and down in a futile attempt to trigger a quake. The Earthquake Awareness Task Force gave out the wrong toll-free number and all calls went instead to a travel agent in California.

By the end of that day the biggest nonevent in Missouri history faded, and news crews went back to their newspapers and radio and television stations with nothing more than

The Hunter-Dawson Home in New Madrid

the news that nothing happened. The man who created the whole thing, Iben Browning, didn't return phone calls that night.

A large dike running the length of town protects New Madrid's historic buildings from the Mississippi River. Here the Mississippi makes almost a 360-degree turn, bringing part of Kentucky almost into New Madrid's lap.

The town now seems most proud of several antebellum homes. One of these, the Hunter-Dawson Home, is a state historic site and is open for viewing. It was built in 1858 and 1859 with slave labor and St. Louis craftsmen, and it has been restored to its original appearance. Another is the Bloomfield Home, more than 150 years old and the oldest brick home in the area. Another of these mansions, known as the A. B. Hunter Sr. Mansion, now houses the New Madrid County

Health Center. The New Madrid Historical Museum is on Main Street and has displays related to all major events in the town's history.

New Madrid is a short distance off I-55, which heads north to Sikeston to complete this loop trip.

In the Area

Towosahgy State Historic Site and Big Oak Tree State Park (East Prairie): 314-649-3149

New Madrid Historical Museum (New Madrid): 314-748-5944

7 ~

Scenic

Highway

19

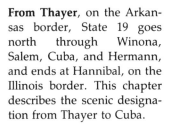

From Thayer, on the Arkansas border, State 19 goes north through Winona, Salem, Cuba, and Hermann, and ends at Hannibal, on the Illinois border. This chapter describes the scenic designation from Thayer to Cuba.

Highlights: *Seven of America's largest springs, disappearing rivers, the Ozark National Scenic Riverways, gristmills, and winding roads through beautiful hardwood forests.*

State 19 is one of Missouri's most beautiful highways and goes through one of the state's most geologically interesting areas. The entire highway, from Thayer to Hannibal, is worth traveling. Several years ago I turned off I-44 at Cuba and drove north on State 19 to Hermann, but I don't trust my memory to describe this section of the highway. I do remember noting how beautiful the Bourbeuse River was near the bridge I crossed, because trees hung down into the slow water, and somewhere along the route—Drake, perhaps?—I saw a very large old general store building with either antiques or old junk—I can't always tell one from the other—on the long porch.

The section under discussion here, from Thayer to Cuba, is special to most Missourians. There's hardly anyone in the state who hasn't paddled a canoe or rowed a boat down the Jacks Fork, Current River, or the Eleven Point River, or planned to or at least wanted to. But I'm getting ahead of myself.

The highway begins at Thayer, right on the Missouri-Arkansas line. Thayer merges with Mammoth Spring just south of the border. The spring is part of the large system of underground rivers and resulting springs that make this area so interesting. Some riverbeds are caves, and several streams can suddenly disappear into the earth and follow an underground route until they emerge again as a spring. This underground network is what caused the gorge at Grand Gulf State Park, six miles west of Thayer. More than a mile of a cave's ceiling collapsed and created this gorge with walls up to 130 feet high. One section of the ceiling remains standing as a natural bridge. The gorge is sometimes called the "Little Grand Canyon." The area is open for visitors, but the park is still being developed, so facilities are modest at best.

This part of Missouri is almost entirely limestone, and it is laced with caves of all sizes. This is because limestone erodes so easily that a cross section of the earth's surface here would look like a honeycomb. Some of these caves are very large, and many have been turned into tourist attractions, such as the more than thirty caves in Meramec State Park, in addition to Marvel Cave near Branson, Mark Twain Cave, those in Ha Ha Tonka State Park, and Onondaga caverns. The largest collection of caves is in Perry County between Ste. Genevieve and Cape Girardeau. At the last count I read, Perry County had 629 caves of all sizes.

In fact, only Tennessee has more known caves, which must be a lot because in 1990 the Missouri Department of Natural Resources recorded the 5,000th cave. Governor John Ashcroft immediately declared 1990 as "The Year of the Cave."

Stop in at a country store

This number is undoubtedly larger now because the department says that for the past thirty-five years an average of
140 caves have been discovered annually throughout the
state.

I hope you didn't buy this book assuming you would
read about the inside of caves, because I don't like them and
have gone into them only under protest from companions or
children, and threats from editors who sent me to them. This
has forced me into caves in Spain, Greece, and Arizona, as
well as Missouri. I have had to go into mines on assignment
as a reporter, including an icy mine on Baffin Island in the
Arctic. I probably heard the stories of people perishing in
caves and mines too many times while growing up. They
scare me and I no longer seek out new and interesting ways to
be scared.

While driving between Thayer and Winona I saw more garage sales and flea markets than anywhere else in Missouri. My search for a used percolator, which started back near St. Joseph, was a leitmotif of the trip, and it was just north of Thayer that I almost settled for a battered teakettle, but I remained true to the quest.

Eleven Point River flows under State 19 north of Greer, and it is Missouri's only designated Wild and Scenic River. A mile-long trail leads back to Greer Spring, another of the large springs in the Ozarks.

This is an area I remember from a summer during my high school years when I worked with a surveyor who had a contract with the Rural Electrification Agency to survey for electrical power lines all through the area. Part of the time we were in the Irish Wilderness area—the most remote place I had ever been. We took the truck as far as we could, then walked the rest of the way. We drove stakes for poles in some of the thickest brush I had ever seen. I was the chain man, meaning I dragged the measuring chain, which also meant I was at the bottom of the survey crew pecking order. I was also responsible for clearing brush between my boss and his transit and the man holding the rod. I worked as hard as a wood-cutter in the Yukon.

We occasionally went past a house that no car or truck could reach because there was no road to it, only the twin ruts of iron-tired wagons. While we were working our way past one of these houses, a buxom girl about my age came out to watch us, and my boss told me that I was not to speak to her or even look at her. "Her daddy has a big gun just sitting there waiting to be used on someone like you," my boss said. I looked anyway. When you're sixteen, hormones are more powerful than brains.

Eminence is the center of the Ozark National Scenic Riverways, which covers about 135 miles of the Current River and Jacks Fork, which enters the Current a short distance below Eminence. The national park begins at Montauk State Park, where the Current River emerges from underground. The other branch begins just upstream from Blue Spring on Jacks Fork. The park ends several miles downriver from Van Buren.

The national park has more than sixty springs, including the appropriately named Big Spring, believed to be the largest single-outlet spring in the world; 286 million gallons of water come out of it every day. Other large springs include Alley Spring, where a two-story water-powered roller mill still stands.

These rivers created a demand for a boat built especially for them, and the result was long and narrow with a flat bottom for clearing the shallows. The design that lasted was called a johnboat, in honor of the man who developed it for the White River. Trouble is, nobody can remember John's last name.

In the late 1970s, a group of high school students from Lebanon, Missouri, working under the auspices of a magazine called *Bittersweet*, watched and helped a boatbuilder named Emmitt Massey construct a johnboat.

"Originally," Massey told them, "they were built right on the riverbank . . . They were long. I've heard of some as long as twenty-seven feet to haul freight on the Current River. They were designed to be stable enough to stand upright in while fishing and to float in four inches of water."

Today few of the wooden johnboats remain. Aluminum has taken over because these boats are much lighter, more durable than wood, and cheaper to build. Several boatbuilding factories are scattered through the Ozarks, keeping the price down and availability high.

Canoes are more popular than johnboats with visitors to the national park, and in all towns in the area you'll see stacks of canoes, looking almost like firewood, for rent. Nearby will

Canoe the riverways

be a school bus of middle or old age that the rental firm uses to take customers to the river, and to bring them back from the river when they're through with their boat trip.

One thing I forgot to ask about. Years ago when we made camp coffee simply by boiling it in a pot without benefit of strainers or filters, we called it Current River coffee. I wonder if it is still called that.

State 19 earns its scenic designation as it winds its way along the creeks and over the ridges to Salem. It is a great highway for sports cars, but not so great for anyone prone to carsickness, because it is almost entirely double yellow lined, if not for curves, for steep hills. The highway is lined with large blackjack and white oak, and in some places the trees form a canopy overhead. A few areas near the road have been logged over, but a screen of trees was left along the highway, easing the visual impact considerably. I must admit that I am like many people who love to use wood—for fires in the fireplace and for furniture—but I dislike seeing areas that have been logged over so I can have that wood. It is something like the lover of steaks who says slaughterhouses should be closed.

In Salem, a pretty town with lots of brick homes and a four-story courthouse, I saw a sign that told me where I was: It read, "Parking out back." On the West Coast the sign would have said, "Parking in the rear." This reminded me of the surprise I had while studying Chaucer in college. I found some expressions in his *Canterbury Tales* that my mother often used. While visiting with my siblings recently, we went over several expressions from the Ozarks that none of us had heard elsewhere. I still use some of these words, which my children sometimes think are quaint, and sometimes they think I'm being "hicky": fur piece means a long way, lolly-gag means to loaf, ear bobs are earrings, tetched means crazy, proud can mean glad, jump the broomstick means to get married.

And my wonderful late mother would never, never call a male cow a bull. It was always male cow. I distinctly remember being told to never use the word *bull* anytime, anywhere. I don't think male horses were called studs either; they were stallions or male horses. I'm still not certain if I am being vulgar when I say bull or stud.

North of Salem about twenty-three miles is the very small town of Cherryville, with a very large stone schoolhouse. Here you can turn east on State 49 and drive about twelve miles down to the Dillard Mill State Historic Site. It is a pretty drive to the odd little town of Dillard, with only three or four homes, one with enough machinery parts out front to stock a parts store and the others as neat as this one is casual. It looked as though the other homeowners might be excessively neat to compensate for the one that wasn't.

The mill is a mile from town on a dirt road that quickly becomes red clay, which made me happy that I wasn't visiting there in the rainy season. The road winds along the banks of Huzzah Creek, and passes a few farms and a small cemetery before arriving at the mill.

Dillard Mill, which looks like an enormous red barn from a distance, was one of the last of the Missouri gristmills to go out of business. It was still grinding flour and meal until the 1960s because the area remained reasonably isolated. The original mill was built sometime before the Civil War and was known as the Wisdom Mill for its owner, Francis Wisdom, who later sold it to Joseph Dillard Cotrell, whose middle name was selected as a name for the community, which later gave way to Davisville.

The next owner was Emil Mischke, who immigrated with his sister Mary from Poland. He bought the property and in 1904 began building the present mill, using some timbers from the old mill. He blasted the millrace out of the limestone bluff and used a turbine rather than a waterwheel.

Mary Mischke became a partner in 1907, then sold back to her brother ten years later. Emil worked alone for another decade but didn't like it, so he got himself a mail-order bride. This was the time of World War I and Missouri had many German immigrants, but after World War I anti-German sentiment ran high. His wife had never liked life in the Ozarks, so when some of his neighbors questioned Mischke's loyalty, he sold the mill to Lester E. Klemme in 1930, moved to California, and never returned.

Klemme built rental cabins on the site and turned it into a resort called Klemme's Old Mill Lodge. He offered fishing in the millpond, and included meals in the $7 per day charge. He operated the mill for nearly thirty years before shutting it down for good in the 1960s. The state acquired the property, added several picnic areas, and offers guided tours throughout the year.

Back on State 19, you'll cross the Meramec River just north of Steelville. When you look down from the bridge on this free-flowing stream, think of all the Missourians who went to battle with the Corps of Engineers several years ago when the Corps not only announced they were going to dam the river, they had started construction before opponents were able to stop the proceedings. The Meramec is as pretty as the Eleven Point River and the more widely promoted rivers in the Ozark National Scenic Riverways. It runs along high limestone bluffs and through timber and open fields on its way to the Mississippi just south of St. Louis.

This journey ends at I-44 in Cuba, but feel free to continue north to the Missouri River at Hermann or the Mississippi at Hannibal to connect with routes described in other chapters.

In the Area

Ozark National Scenic Riverways (Van Buren):
314-323-4236

Dillard Mill State Historic Site (Davisville):
314-244-3120

8 ~

Missouri's Route du Vin

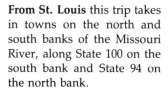

From St. Louis this trip takes in towns on the north and south banks of the Missouri River, along State 100 on the south bank and State 94 on the north bank.

Highlights: *Missouri's major wine district; historic towns of Washington, Hermann, Labadie, St. Albans; lots of bed and breakfasts; European-style festivals.*

I am partial to trips that begin in a large city without having to drive white-knuckled down an interstate highway amid drivers who know where they're going when I don't. So one afternoon I landed at Lambert Field, picked up a rental car, and drove into St. Louis for a quick look at the downtown area after an absence of several years, then meandered out Manchester Boulevard and just kept going. Just beyond the city limits Manchester drops by the wayside and State 100 takes over and doesn't stop until you're almost in Jefferson City. I've never driven any farther west on State 100 than Hermann, but that is sufficient, indeed.

Because of its deep ties with Germany, the region has become known as Missouri's Rhineland. It is a good name because a touch of the Old World is strung out along the last 100 miles of the Missouri River before it joins the Mississippi in St. Louis. Oak and walnut trees cover the low hills, and row crops march across the rich bottomlands. Towns with sturdy buildings made of limestone and brick perch on the high bluffs along the southern bank of the river. Lutheran churches are usually as tall as the Catholic competition, and homes and businesses are so well built that it would take a very large bomb to demolish them.

Little known outside of Missouri until lately, this is one of the major winemaking areas of the Midwest. Some of the oldest wineries in America were established here. In one of those oddities of history, wine grapes grown here were responsible, in a negative way, for changing the entire French wine industry.

Hermann is the focal point of the Rhineland. Other German-settled towns stand farther west, such as Starkenburg and Westphalia, and ethnographic maps of Missouri show German settlements all over the state, but Hermann represents the most ambitious attempt to retain nineteenth-century German culture. Lately it has been the most active in promoting the preservation of Missouri's German heritage, and more than 100 of its buildings are on the National Register, which is most of the buildings in the small town of less than 3,000 population.

Hermann was founded in 1837 by members of the Philadelphia Settlement Society, an organization of German immigrants who set out to establish a colony in the remote west that would carry out the ideals of German nationalism. The society bought 11,000 acres in Missouri and sold off lots to its members. These newcomers were so well educated that locals nicknamed them the Lateinische Bauern, "Latin Peasants."

This learning is reflected in names they gave the town and its streets. Hermann was named in honor of Hermann Arminius, the German warrior whose armies defeated Caesar Augustus's forces in the Battle of Teutoburg in the year A.D. 9, and forced them back from the Elbe River to the Rhine. Hermann settlers named streets after Mozart, Beethoven, Goethe, Gutenberg, and Schiller; when they laid out the town, they made the main street wider than Philadelphia's main boulevard.

Grapes were one of the first crops they planted because they found that the soil and climate were similar to that of their homeland. The first grapes matured in 1845, and in 1846 the vineyards produced 1,000 gallons of wine. Soon wine was the major product in the area, and by 1893 Stone Hill Winery in Hermann was the third largest winery in the world. The largest was in Europe, the second largest was the Lonz Winery in Ohio.

Then came the chain of events that had such an impact on the wine industry in Europe and America in the late nineteenth century. It started when wines from Missouri began overshadowing European wines at international competitions; during the 1851 Vienna World's Fair, for example, Missouri wines took eight of the twelve gold medals. To fight fire with fire, French vintners began importing rootstock from America, mainly the Norton/Cynthiana vines, which were producing most of the award winners.

Nobody knew until it was almost too late that the American vines carried a root louse called phylloxera. The tiny pest, no larger than a grass seed, had no effect on vines in the Ozarks, but once in France it began systematically destroying the vineyards. The plague spread across France, and by 1880 nearly all French vineyards were either destroyed or severely damaged.

Many farmers assumed that their career in the wine industry was over, and they began growing other crops that required less of an investment of money and time; wheat and nearly all vegetable crops are much easier to grow than wine grapes, which require an enormous amount of work—something like having a sickly child. The plague threatened to cross boundaries into other countries, but then a Missouri winemaker named Hermann Jaeger and a University of Missouri professor named George Hussman found a cure for the plague by grafting the more sensitive vines onto hardy American rootstocks that were already immune. These two men literally saved the French wine industry. The episode also radically changed the way the French thereafter produced wine.

When Jaeger and Hussman proved that their new strains were immune to the plague, the French imported an estimated 10 million rootstocks between 1885 and 1890 and replanted their vineyards. Since most large vineyards had already been consigned to grow other crops, the smaller vineyards became much more specialized. Quality and individuality became more important than quantity. Consequently, French wines became better than ever before.

The French were grateful for the Missouri rootstocks, and in 1889 bestowed the Cross of the Legion of Honor and the national Order of Knighthood on Hermann Jaeger. A statue of a young woman holding an older woman—symbolic of the young America helping an older France—was erected on the campus of an agricultural college in Montpellier, France, with a plaque thanking the Missouri wine industry for saving the French vineyards.

Today Missouri winemakers are especially fond of telling what happened when California needed a supply of rootstock after its vineyards began dying of the root louse. Rather than going to Missouri for their supply, they imported the Missouri-born rootstocks from France. Somehow, having to say their vines came from Missouri (shudder) was too grim to contemplate, Missourians like to say.

The Talcoa winery in California's Napa Valley hired George Hussman to work his magic. He later owned his own winery, the Oak Glen, in the Chiles Valley until he died in 1902. In 1891, two years after receiving the Cross of the Legion of Honor, Hermann Jaeger left his home in southwest Missouri, saying he was going to Joplin. But he left a note asking his family not to look for him. He was never seen again.

Like wineries everywhere in America, those in Missouri suffered a severe blow when Prohibition put an end to commercial winemaking in the 1930s. All of Hermann's wineries closed; Stone Hill was converted to growing mushrooms. It continued doing so until 1965, when a local couple, Jim and Betty Held, bought the whole operation, got rid of the mushrooms, and began making wine again. Today Stone Hill is

Vineyards

perhaps the best known of Hermann's wineries; it stands on a high hill overlooking Hermann and the Missouri River. Founded in 1847, it has a series of cellars, supposedly the largest in America, shown on tours. The tasting room sells wine, gifts, and food items. The winery also has the Vintage 1847 Restaurant, which is open for lunch and dinner.

Downtown on Hermann's main street is another winery, the Hermanhoff, established in 1852, five years after Stone Hill. A National Historic Site, it has a large main building and the Festhalle, said to be the world's largest wine hall. Tours show the ten stone and brick arched cellars and the smokehaus where German sausages are made. Picnickers are welcome in the courtyard. Next door is an Amish Country Store with handmade gifts.

Several of Hermann's beautiful homes built by vintners before Prohibition have been turned into bed and breakfasts. The largest is the three-story Victorian brick mansion called Birk's Goethe Street Gasthaus, which was built by the owner of Stone Hill Winery. Elmer and Gloria Birk have worked several years restoring and furnishing the home, and are still making small improvements to put it back in its original condition. They have made a specialty of mystery weekends, which run Friday through Sunday on the first two full weekends of each month. Reservations well in advance are essential for the mystery weekends, and recommended at other times.

Another popular bed and breakfast is the Schmidt Guesthouse, owned by Mimi Schmidt, who helped found the annual Maifest in 1952, and who now is director of Hermann's Showboat community theater. Her bed and breakfast is small—only two to four guests—and intimate, and she enjoys showing guests around the town of her birth.

Hermann also has the distinction of having the only courthouse in Missouri built with private funds. When a local wealthy citizen named Charles D. Eitzen died, he left $50,000 to build the Gasconade County Courthouse.

Hermann has several celebrations throughout the year, and is well equipped for large crowds; its Beer Hall is said to be the largest in the world. The major festivals are the Wurstfest the third weekend of March, the Maifest on the third weekend of May, the annual antique market on the third weekend of June, the Great Stone Hill Grape Stomp the second Saturday of August, the Volksmarch on the third weekend of September, the Octoberfest every weekend in October, and an old-fashioned Christmas celebration in December.

Wine has become more and more important in Missouri's Rhineland, and about a dozen wineries are scattered within sight of the Missouri River between Hermann and St. Louis. Oddly, the relatively small region supports two viticultural areas, Hermann and Augusta. The latter was the first such area designated in America after the U.S. Treasury Department established the system in 1983. Interestingly, Missouri grapes are still not affected by phylloxera, which at this writing is again killing grapevines in the Napa Valley.

Although Hermann is the centerpiece of the Rhineland, the rest of the area on both sides of the Missouri down to St. Louis has good restaurants, inns, and bed and breakfasts, and of course several wineries. At the urging of Elmer Birk, I stopped at the Bias Winery a short distance downriver from Hermann at Berger. The winery came about almost by accident. Jim Bias, an airline pilot, and his wife, Norma, were looking for a country place within driving distance of the airport in St. Louis. They found one near Berger and bought the place for its location. When told that the property included a vineyard, they had a so-what attitude, until they found that the grapes had been growing in the area since 1843. That piqued their interest, and it wasn't long before the friendly, unpretentious couple was producing excellent wine that attracted the favorable attention of President Reagan and various national wine critics. Visitors may tour the vineyard on golf carts and have a picnic beside a pond where ducks and geese beg.

About half a dozen wineries are on the north side of the Missouri, from St. Louis to the small town of Portland northwest of Hermann on State 94. (You can cross the river on State 19 in Hermann, then head west on State 94 to Portland.) The Green Valley Vineyards, in Portland, makes wine from fifteen acres of French hybrid grapes and specializes in dry and semidry wines.

Blumenhof Vineyards is in Dutzow, a picturesque town downriver on State 94 with rolling hills and steep timber. The vineyard specializes in dry table wines.

A short distance downriver is Augusta, one of those little places that sat virtually ignored for decades until the Rhineland started coming into its own. Augusta was built on the bank of the Missouri, but one spring many years ago the river shifted its course two miles away and stayed there. The funky, ramshackle little town was left high and dry on a low hill overlooking rich bottomland. One of the towns damaged by the 1993 flooding, Augusta has become an arts-and-crafts center and has three wineries: Mount Pleasant, Cedar Ridge, and Montelle.

Augusta's vineyards have the distinction of being the first area in the United States to be granted an appellation when the Department of Agriculture created the appellation system modeled after those in France.

To visit more of the Rhineland on the south side of the river, cross back over it again on State 19 into Hermann, then head east on State 100. A few miles outside Washington is the Sunny Slope Winery in a brick home that dates back to the

Civil War. The winery is set in the vineyard where French hybrid grapes are grown.

Farther down the Missouri River toward St. Louis are other wineries and historic towns. Most of Washington sits on a bluff even higher than Hermann. Beautiful buildings range from the sturdy German-design brick and stone to the Victorian mansions on the hills. For nearly a century the town has been known for two factories: one that made excellent zithers around the turn of the century, and the other that has turned out millions of corncob pipes. The Missouri Meerschaum Co. opened for business in 1869. The company was Gen. Douglas MacArthur's sole supplier of the distinctive pipes with a four-and-a-half-inch tall bowl and long stem. Other famous customers were Gen. John J. "Blackjack" Pershing, President Gerald Ford, President Dwight D. Eisenhower, and Carl Sandburg.

The pipes are made from a type of corn developed by the University of Missouri to produce a thick, tough cob, and the company contracts with several farmers to grow the cobs for them. The farmers get to keep the corn and are paid per acre of cobs grown. This guarantees the company a steady supply of cobs so they can keep their production at an average of 7,000 pipes per day.

Most of Washington's riverfront buildings have been restored and turned into offices, shops, and restaurants. Although Washington is very hilly—all towns on the south side of the river are—it is a pleasant town for walking.

Some of the towns along this stretch of the river have remained small, hardly more than a cluster of buildings. Labadie is a row of Victorian homes and false-front store buildings. St. Albans, one of the oldest towns in the state, is near a cave described at some length by Lewis and Clark in the journals from their 1804–6 journey to the Pacific. It was near here that Captain Lewis nearly fell off a 300-foot cliff and barely managed to catch himself after falling about 20 feet. All of St. Albans's few buildings are elegant in a turn-of-the-century way, and all, including the post office, are owned by one family.

One of the nicest characteristics of Missouri's Rhineland is that the area has a lived-in look: it isn't a series of villages with a theme painted on them to attract visitors. You will share the narrow highways with tractors pulling manure spreaders, and a few farmers still use horses for some field work. When you go into a hardware store you will find nuts and bolts, barbed wire, ten-penny nails, horseshoe nails, and axle grease. You probably won't find postcards and T-shirts. At the post office you'll see groups of men in overalls and gum boots standing around talking about catawba grapes and chenin blanc as though wine is just another local product, like corn or hay. Which, of course, it is.

In the Area

More information on Missouri wines is available in the brochure "Taste Missouri Wine Country": Grape and Wine Program, P.O. Box 630, Jefferson City, MO 65102. 314-751-6807

Hermann Area Chamber of Commerce (Hermann): 314-486-2313

Washington Area Chamber of Commerce (Washington): 314-239-2715

Birk's Gasthaus (Hermann): 800-748-7883 or 314-486-2911

9 ~

Arrow Rock to Fort Osage

From I-70 at Boonville, in central Missouri, take State 41 west to Marshall, then west to US 24 into Lexington.

Highlights: *Historic Arrow Rock and Lexington, one of Missouri's major Civil War battlefields, and Fort Osage.*

This trip is a good alternative to cruising across Missouri on I-70 sandwiched between semis going seventy-five miles an hour. The distance between Boonville and Kansas City on this route isn't that much greater than on I-70, but the traveling conditions are much better. This route offers rolling hills with alternating timber and crops, and two historic towns.

The area around Boonville is rich in Indian and Civil War history, and a small town northwest of Boonville named Arrow Rock is one of the most historically interesting towns in the area, in part because it still looks so much like it did when it came into being. Arrow Rock is one of the earliest landmarks noted by explorers on the Missouri River. The first maps were by French cartographers who called the landmark Pierre à Fleche, for the very good reason that it means arrow rock in French. They apparently heard it called that by Indians in the area who used its stone for arrowheads. It was such a distinct landmark that everyone who went by mentioned it in writing, including the Lewis and Clark expedition in 1804.

The first trading post was established in 1813 by George Sibley, who abandoned it a year later due to the increase in Indian raids. He and his wife went downriver to St. Charles and founded Lindenwood College. Although Sibley's Fort and Trading Post didn't last long, it was an impressive structure. It was of traditional blockhouse design with a two-story main building that measured twenty feet by thirty feet. It was made of cottonwood logs with an oak slab roof. A log stockade surrounded it.

Arrow Rock became more busy as the route from St. Charles west became a trail, then a road called Boone's Lick (or Booneslick) Road. It ran to Old Franklin, across the river from where Boonville stands now. This became the launching pad for the Santa Fe Trail, which was started by William Becknell when he made a round-trip to Santa Fe in forty-eight days. This trail began at Old Franklin, went upriver a short distance to Arrow Rock, then left the river and turned north on a long loop, and headed straight for Fort Osage near Independence. Here the Santa Fe, California, and Oregon Trails converged, then went their separate ways again. In later years the Santa Fe Trail officially began downriver at Independence, 780 miles from Santa Fe.

All of this became history once the transcontinental railroads were built. Like nearly every town that depended on trails, Arrow Rock became only a shadow of its former self.

In 1873 Arrow Rock was partly destroyed by a fire set by three young arsonists, who were arrested, then lynched

Arrow Rock Tavern

before a trial could be held. Another fire struck in 1901 that caused extensive damage to the downtown district.

Arrow Rock has remained small and historic. The restoration program began when the Daughters of the American Revolution took on the Old Tavern as a project in 1912. A decade later the Missouri Legislature purchased the tavern so the DAR could continue its restoration, which in turn led to the creation of Arrow Rock State Park in 1926. The park was further improved in the 1930s by a Works Progress Administration project.

The Friends of Arrow Rock was formed in 1959 and raised funds to restore the Old Courthouse, the IOOF Lodge Hall, the Gun Shop, and some other buildings. Nearly every building in town has a name and its history in print. One of the most popular buildings is the home of the great Missouri painter George Caleb Bingham, from when he built it in 1837 until he moved away in 1845. He was a very popular portrait painter among his neighbors; one source said, "Not to have a Bingham on the wall was as rare as not to have a Bible on the center table." The house, at the end of High Street, was declared a National Historic Landmark in 1968, after being restored by the Missouri Park Department.

Next door to the Bingham house is a large depression in the bluff that separates the town from the Missouri River. It is called Godsey's Diggin's in honor of the man in charge of a public works project that was never completed. The town fathers decided to dig a channel from the river into the heart of town so that wharves and warehouses would be easier served by riverboats and barges. The work continued off and on from 1840 until 1857, but the town has only the man-made ravine to show for the project.

The Lyceum Theater, Missouri's oldest professional theater, performs a selection of musicals, comedies, and dramas through the summer, and the town has the usual assortment of bed and breakfasts, restaurants, antique stores, and gift shops. Fortunately, most of the downtown buildings have a lived-in look rather than a perfectly preserved façade.

As you've no doubt noticed, writing this book has put me into something of an A. E. Housman mode of remembering things from my youth, but without the sadness or regrets of brooks too broad for leaping. One of my favorite memories from this area is from the year and a half I attended the University of Missouri in Columbia. It isn't one of those grand adventures I use to bore my children and is nothing more or less than a wonderful Sunday afternoon.

The historical Lyceum Theater in Arrow Rock

For a short time I lived in the Delta Chi fraternity house, which later had the distinction of being the only house on Greek Row with a president on academic probation. After I moved to Seattle the house was closed down by the university, which tells you something of its quality. However, the few months I lived in the house I made some friendships that have lasted through the years, including a New Zealander named Philip V. Harkness, who was in America to study journalism.

I didn't own a car—I had sold mine to pay my tuition at St. Louis University the previous year—but Phil owned a 1949 Ford, which he loaned me from time to time, in part I'm sure because I worked at Bob Jones's Standard Oil service station and I took very good care of the car.

One winter Sunday, Phil, a lovely girl from Branson, and I drove up to visit a fraternity brother, John Lawrence, Jr., the son of a prominent physician who practiced in Marshall. The Lawrences lived in an enormous home with a fireplace in every room. It still stands—on County TT just west of Arrow Rock—and is known as the Sappington House. It was built by Dr. John Sappington, of Arrow Rock, who invented Sappington Anti-fever Pills, using quinine as a cure for malaria, one of the most common ailments in those years. Sappington later gave away rights to the pills rather than collecting a royalty. One of Sappington's grandsons became governor of Missouri and two of his sons-in-law held that office.

Behind the house were several small huts that had been slave quarters; I am told that only one of these remains today.

Our afternoon wasn't a historical event, and I don't remember the young woman's name. I saw Phil in New Zealand a few years ago and he remembered that day with the same warmth. Neither of us has seen John since about 1958. We had a wonderful time on that cold winter afternoon talking with John in the library and enjoying the winter sunlight coming through the tall windows. This was about the time I first became acquainted with the paintings of William M. Harnett, and I remember seeing tools and a barn jacket on pegs on a wall that needed only a pheasant hanging there to make it a Harnett scene. John's mother served lunch, we went for a walk across the cold and barren fields, then drove back to Columbia. A perfect winter Sunday.

It wasn't too far from Arrow Rock that I had another memorable November afternoon. It was a year later and a friend and I borrowed shotguns from a farmer and hunted quail on his land. We didn't have a dog, so we took turns walking through blackberry thickets to flush the birds. On one of my turns, I walked into the thicket, shotgun held high with both hands to avoid being scratched, and suddenly three or four quail shot out of the vines to my right. My friend was standing to my left, and I saw his shotgun swinging my way. I dove facedown into the berry vines just as he fired over my head. I assumed that he fired where my head would have been. I got up, face and hands scratched, and I haven't hunted since.

State 41 continues on to Marshall, a small city of about 12,000 population with an emphasis on manufacturing and agriculture. The route to Lexington is west on US 65 to Waverly, then west on US 24, which continues through Lexington to Kansas City.

Lexington is a town of about 5,000 with a rich history that comes from a three-day Civil War battle that ended on September 20, 1861. The town was founded by migrants from Lexington, Kentucky; when the Civil War broke out it was an important river port. Most of the citizens had pro-South leanings, but all doubts of allegiance were erased when the Union soldiers came to town in September 1861 and took nearly $1 million from the local bank.

A few days later the Missouri Guard arrived and the Battle of Lexington began. A cannonball from the battle is still lodged in the east column of the courthouse. This battle, considered one of the major battles fought in Missouri, was between the Missouri State Guard under the command of Maj. Gen. Sterling Price and the Union troops under Col. James A. Mulligan.

Some call the conflict the Battle of Hemp Bales because bales of the material were used as breastworks. The Anderson House, now a museum, was used as a field hospital by both sides at various times as it changed hands during the battle.

After the battle ended, General Price reported that his men had captured five pieces of artillery, 100 wagons, 300 muskets, and about 1,000 horses, and recovered $900,000 of the money taken from the bank.

The Battle of Lexington State Historic Park is just outside of town. Trenches and earthworks from the battle have been preserved, and a mile-long interpretive trail tells the story.

About eleven miles south of Lexington on State 13 is the Confederate Memorial, a 100-acre park with the Old Confederate Soldiers' Home, commemorating the 40,000 Missourians who died for the Confederate cause.

US 24 and State 224 parallel each other along the Missouri River, and finally State 224 disappears at Napoleon. At Buckner, turn north on County BB to Sibley, where Fort Osage has been reconstructed. The first mention of the site is in the journals of Lewis and Clark. Clark camped there on June 23, 1804, on the way west. He had gone ahead of the party to hunt and had killed a deer. Here, in his engaging writing style with adventurous spelling, is what happened next:

> I Killed a Deer & made a fire, expecting the boat would come up in the evening. the wind continuing to blow prevented their moving, as the distance by land was too great for me to return by night I concluded to Camp, Peeled Some bark to lay on, and geathered

wood to make fired to keep off musquiturs & knats. Heard the party on Shore fire, at Dark Drewyer came to me with the horses, one fat bear & a Deer, river fell 8 Inches last night.
Set out at half after Six [the next day]. I joined the boat this morng at 8 oClock (I will only remark that dureing the time I lay on the sand waiting for the boat, a large Snake Swam to the bank imediately under the Deer which was hanging over the water, and no great distance from it, I threw chunks and drove this snake off Several times. I found that he was so determined on getting to the meet I was compelld to kill him, the part of the Deer which attracted this Snake I think was the Milk from the bag of the Doe.)

By 1808, Clark was territorial governor and Fort Osage was built under his direction as the first U.S. outpost in the Louisiana Purchase. It was built as a trading post with the Indians, but also to serve notice to the Spanish, British, and Indians that the United States meant business with the Louisiana Purchase.

The fort was eventually destroyed, and its ruins lay ignored for more than a century. In the early 1970s the Friends of Fort Osage was created, which joined forces with the town of Sibley and the Jackson County Historical Society to rebuild the fort. It was declared a National Monument in the early 1980s and was given a federal grant. The restoration was completed in 1986 and the fort was taken over by Jackson County Parks and Recreation. It has a blacksmith shop and exhibits of trade goods. A living-history program conducts tours and special holiday candlelight programs.

From Sibley you can return to US 24 the way you came or follow a county road along the Missouri River into Independence.

In the Area

Arrow Rock State Historic Site and Park (Arrow Rock):
816-837-3330

Historic Arrow Rock Council (Arrow Rock): 816-837-3470

Lexington Chamber of Commerce (Lexington): 816-259-2040

Battle of Lexington State Historic Site (Lexington):
816-259-4654

Fort Osage County Park (Sibley): 816-881-4431

10 ~

The Heart of the Ozarks

From West Plains, in south-central Missori, take US 160 west to Branson.

Highlights: *Ozark scenery, crafts, gristmills, lakes, Shepherd of the Hills country, Branson area.*

This chapter is the hardest to write because this is my home country. I was born about two miles off US 160 and went through high school in West Plains. I left with memories of the hard life on farms, and when I return today I still remember that kind of endless labor with little return, but without the bitterness so many people carry with them from this kind of life. Now I see the beauty of the Ozarks, perhaps only because I don't have to pick up rocks or chop sprouts, or run traplines before school in the winter, or hoe the garden and saw and chop firewood. That makes a big difference in my attitude.

US 160 runs straight through the Missouri Ozarks, and it touches on the best the region has to offer. Although it begins in Poplar Bluff, two other routes described in this book—State 19 and State 21—cross US 160, so I decided to begin at West Plains and follow the route to its end in Branson.

In recent years this route has become more and more popular with people driving to Branson to see the country and western stars who have built theaters. When I was growing up, we talked a lot about the Shepherd of the Hills country around Lake Taneycomo, Table Rock Lake, Forsyth, and Branson. Most of us who grew up in Ozark County and went to West Plains did so in the back of someone's truck, a privilege for which we paid 25 or 50 cents. Then it was a long and rough ride because the highway wasn't paved until sometime around World War II.

West Plains got its name because it was a treeless area west of Thomasville, a town founded some years earlier on the Eleven Point River. The first known settler in what became West Plains was a hunter who lived around the spring during the summer. He sold his cabin and whatever else he had built to a man from Tennessee named Josiah Howell sometime around 1839.

When the Civil War broke out, West Plains was abandoned to the bands of guerrillas who came through more interested in terrorizing people and burning houses and barns than striking blows for political philosophies. One band led by a man named Watson burned the abandoned homes to the ground. When one citizen returned, the only living thing he found was a cat.

When a railroad was built through town in 1883, West Plains's future was assured, and over the next century it gradually became a trading center for a large section of Missouri and northern Arkansas. Meanwhile, the town grew up around the spring that had helped determine where the town would be built. The post office was built over the spring, and later the building was turned into the public library. You can go into the library today and ask to see the spring and the librarian will oblige.

The town was laid out in the usual fashion, with an East Main Street and a West Main Street. Washington Avenue and St. Louis were the main streets going north; Aid Avenue and South Hill went south. We always called South Hill Standpipe Hill since the city's water tank, or standpipe, stood atop the hill.

The town's dominant feature was, and is, the square, with the Howell County Courthouse in the middle of it. The building took up most of the land allotted to it, but there was room on the north side for a bench or two, and they were occupied by retired men, women resting with their infants, or high school students watching a parade of friends driving by. The jail was on the top floor of the courthouse on the north side, and occasionally the prisoners amused themselves by dumping water on the sitters below.

It is odd, but after all these years West Plains doesn't really have a focal point for me. It has no lasting image that would set it apart from other towns its size. It seemed to have everything a town would need, but nothing extraordinary. I hasten to add that this isn't a criticism, because I know that every town can't have a Civil War site or a row of antebellum mansions, nor can every town be the site of some horrible crime. Instead, West Plains has just been there—stable, pleasant and successful.

US 160 comes into town from the east, goes west on Broadway, then south, ascends a hill, and passes where the Hill Crest dance hall used to stand. I once danced there with a girl who used vanilla extract for perfume; when I said something sarcastic about it to my friends back at the table, one of the girls gave me a stern and memorable lecture, because that was the only thing the girl could afford.

Beyond West Plains, US 160 passes through countryside typical of the Ozarks today—no row crops, only vegetable gardens and fields of hay. The countryside has so many modern homes now that it looks like a suburb with exceptionally wide spacing. I was told that most people work in town and keep the farms for the love of living on them and for having something to do.

It was along this highway that many years ago while going to the University of Missouri I saw a scene that came to represent the Missouri I grew up in. I was driving alone on a summer morning in July or August. The weather was typically hot and humid, and since it was long before air-conditioning was common in cars, I was undoubtedly driving with the windows down. Not far from the highway a man was plowing his field and a single horse was pulling the plow. It had been a while since I had seen that, but suddenly it all came back to me: the smell of the earth, the difficulty of walking with one foot in the soft dirt and the other on firm ground, the hard work of holding the plow at the proper angle while geeing and hawing the horse to keep a straight line. Compound this with the extreme heat and it was a miserable morning.

I slowed up, and before I got alongside the plowman, he had stopped the horse and lifted the lines off his shoulder. Like my father always did, he had tied the lines together and strung one over his left shoulder and the other under his right arm. He dropped the plow on its side and stretched his arms and shoulders. Then he did something I wish I could have photographed. He lifted his head to let the faint breeze cool his neck, but he looked as though he was praying for relief from the hard work and the intense heat. I knew how it felt to wear a cotton shirt under overalls and how much it burned when the overall straps pressed the hot cotton against the shoulders and back.

I also knew that down at one end of the field he had buried a gallon water jug and that the jug was wrapped in wet burlap so the evaporation would keep the water cool, and I knew how the water that came from a spring or a well out of the limestone smelled and tasted and what pulling the corncob stopper from the jug sounded like. And I also knew how the horse smelled and sounded, and I could hear the harness creaking and the trace chains clattering, and I knew that when the day was over and the horse was unharnessed he would shake himself several times, then roll on the ground.

I remember thinking then that no matter how badly things were going at the University of Missouri—I wasn't a memorable student—I had to get a degree and do something besides farm in the Ozarks. When I returned years later I found that virtually nobody farmed anymore. The Ozarks had changed and I had changed, and I was a stranger in a place I no longer understood. It didn't make me feel especially sad or have a sense of loss; it was almost as if someone had moved my home while I was away.

Another thing happened along this highway that I have always remembered. When my father died we had a funeral service for him in the funeral home in West Plains and a graveside service on Howards Ridge. We had a procession of perhaps a dozen cars behind the hearse going down US 160. Every time someone working in the fields or standing outside their house saw the procession, they stopped whatever they were doing and stood silently until we were past, and when a man had on a hat, he took it off.

I thought of all these things when I drove down this highway on an earlier trip. The one- or two-store towns of South Fork and Hocomo came and went by, but at Caulfield I had to turn south on State 101 for a look at Bakersfield, where I lived with my brother during my sophomore year in high school and worked in his service station while he drove a school bus. The tiny town square was still there, and so was the little service station, not much larger than a tollbooth, it seemed. The gully was still beside the station where we drove cars out on a platform and changed the oil and lubricated them—we called them grease jobs then—with a hand-powered grease gun. We saved the oil-soaked fiber oil filters in a barrel and burned them in the woodstove during the winter.

I wanted to drive over toward Norfork Lake and see if I still remembered where the Hog Danger schoolhouse stood. The place got its name many years ago because hogs liked to crawl beneath the schoolhouse and they made a terrible racket down there, snorting and squealing and carrying on. The schoolteacher could hardly teach under these conditions, so he heated water on the woodstove, then poured it through cracks in the floor to flush out the hogs. Thus, Hog Danger.

I didn't go in search of Hog Danger. Instead, I returned to US 160 and continued my westward journey. It is about ten miles to Tecumseh—a store and post office—overlooking the bridge across Norfork Lake. The bridge has been there longer than I've been on earth, and it is one of those many landmarks in a life. Every Fourth of July a community picnic was held here, and it was called, naturally, the Bridge Picnic.

It wasn't far north of here on Norfork River that some of my distant relatives made life miserable for game wardens. This form of enforcement officer was detested by nearly everyone in the hills, even though they were trying to prevent people from killing all the game. They were unsuccessful. When I was growing up, all the big game had been killed off. No bears were left, only an occasional panther; the nearest deer were probably in Colorado. The Ozarks had been cleared by people hunting for meat and ignoring the game laws. An example was these relatives, who once caught a game warden, disarmed him, tied him in a tree, and left him there overnight. There were probably as many jokes about game wardens as city slickers, and baiting the wardens was an accepted form of recreation.

Today Missouri has thousands of deer, and the wild turkey population has increased dramatically. It is such a friendly place for game that even armadillos have begun migrating north from Texas. I know. I saw one flattened on a highway. I don't like their looks any more than I like the looks of opossums.

A short distance west of Tecumseh is County J, which leads two miles south to where I was born: Howards Ridge, named for my maternal grandfather, who ran a mail route on a saddle horse and eventually established a post office. The paved road was added long after we moved away, so now it takes no more than ten minutes to drive down to Howards Ridge. First you pass the Faye cemetery, where my Great-Uncle Jack Satterfield is buried; his headstone reveals that he was killed for his money and that he is "Gone but not forgotten." Then the road crosses Lick Creek, where my brothers and I learned to swim, then climbs a small hill and arrives at Howards Ridge.

Little from my childhood remains. Our forty-acre home place doesn't have any buildings standing, only the walnut trees my parents planted. The cemetery is a showplace for a country cemetery. The little church across the road from it that was built when I was about eight has hardly changed, except that electricity has been added to replace the hissing Coleman gas lanterns.

The one-room schoolhouse is long gone. When school consolidation closed it, the little building was torn down to make way for a new road. My father said that the workmen found that saplings had been used for rafters and the bark was still on them. This schoolhouse was the community center and community church until my parents donated enough land for the little church across the road from the cemetery. Sometimes an itinerant preacher came through and sometimes a local celebrity, such as when Slim Pickins Wilson of

KWTO in Springfield gave a concert. One memory that persists is of the man who gave a performance that included feats of strength, such as having a tug-of-war with several men. His major stunt was breaking several bottles and jars in a wooden box, then taking off his shoes and jumping into the box of broken glass. I remember being frightened and hearing those lanterns hissing as he perched on the edge of the teacher's desk, building his courage. He finally jumped, and didn't cut his feet. I've never understood how he did it.

From Howards Ridge I made a small loop by driving west on County T to Mammoth and on State 5 just south of Gainesville, the seat of Ozark County. Later one of my brothers drove the same route and we both marveled at how many nice houses we saw in a place where only modest houses to wretched shacks stood when we lived there. My other brother and sister visited Howards Ridge earlier, and he said he did something he never expected to do there: he flushed a toilet. We had been away several years and had left before electricity and telephones were brought in; I don't think I even heard of a septic tank until I was out of high school.

Gainesville is one of those towns of less than a thousand population that hardly changes from decade to decade. The courthouse has always been the dominant building and probably always will be. It is one of those county seats where you can go into almost any office and be treated like a good neighbor. The county is small, and somebody in the courthouse will have an answer to nearly any question. I had to have my four and a half acres on Howards Ridge appraised once, and the clerk I talked to suggested I call a real estate agent named Sharp. I did and gave her the property description.

She said she would write up an appraisal and mail it to me within a week. She kept her promise but no invoice was included. I called her and asked for the invoice. "I'm not

Ozark quilter

going to charge you or anybody else for something I can do in five minutes without getting out of my chair," she said cheerfully.

All the countryside I saw between West Plains and Gainesville was what I had always remembered: lots of oak timber mixed with ash and hickory and an occasional dogwood and persimmon, but with thick underbrush. I knew that in this brush I would find blackberries, wild strawberries, wild grapes, and all manner of low-growing plant life, poison ivy included. I also knew that if I went strolling through the underbrush I would bring chiggers and possibly ticks into the motor home. I had been away from poisonous snakes so long that I was afraid I had lost my ability to spot a copperhead in the leaves. I walked with extreme care in a place where fifty years earlier I had walked and run barefooted and with abandon.

This part of the Ozarks is partially flooded with manmade lakes: Norfork, Bull Shoals, Taneycomo, Table Rock. All except Taneycomo are the result of hydroelectric dams built across the border in Arkansas, and all have had more of a positive than negative effect because the land they covered was seldom good for farming, and the vast lakes created a tourist industry. I don't remember when the others were built, but when Norfork Dam was built south of Mountain Home, Arkansas, during World War II, it created a lot of jobs for boys too young to go off to war and men who were too old. All were put to work clearing the timber from the land that would be flooded.

It is about sixty miles from Gainesville to Branson, and according to one economic report a few years ago, this east-west strip along the Arkansas border is expected to grow rapidly, thanks in part to the interest Branson has brought to the Ozarks.

There's a tendency toward gentrification of the Ozarks as more money is brought in. More and more large cattle operations have come in—I can't yet bring myself to speak of cattle ranches in the Ozarks because I think ranches stop at about the Colorado-Kansas border in spite of the abundance of cowboy hats and boots made of snakeskin and wildebeest skin. The core of America's large cities may be getting poorer and poorer, but the countryside seems to be getting wealthier. The lakes have brought employment for tourism, construction, hunting, fishing, and all the service industries involved.

US 160 becomes more beautiful the farther west you drive. More and more steep hills have panoramic views of the timbered hills, and you'll find several lovely spots along the shore of Bull Shoals Lake near Sundown, Theodosia, and Ocie. Just beyond here is the beginning of the Shepherd of the Hills area, named for a famous novel by that title written by Harold Bell Wright and published in 1907.

In a sense the novel created this part of Missouri, much as Mark Twain created Hannibal. The novel was made into a silent film and later a successful talkie. For most of this century people have gone to the Shepherd of the Hills country to see Inspiration Point, the Shepherd of the Hills Homestead, and other places Wright wrote about. The novel was deeply religious in tone—Wright was an ordained minister and preached at many churches throughout the area—and the novel became an immediate success. Wright's fans visited the area he wrote about, and souvenir hunters stripped a house that was featured in the book, thus proving that today's fans are no different than their ancestors.

Not all writers about the Ozarks have been so universally loved. One notable exception was a minister named Guy Howard, who wrote a biographical book called *The Walking Preacher of the Ozarks*. The book was published sometime

A Branson fiddler

around World War II and it wasn't very complimentary about residents of the Ozarks.

But another writer, Vance Randolph, who was universally loved, wrote about nothing other than the Ozarks, and lived there most of his adult life. Randolph was a folklorist, and he recorded stories, music, and the way people spoke. He lived in Galena and Pineville, Missouri, and also across the border in Arkansas at Eureka Springs and Fayetteville. He was to Ozarks folklore what Alan Lomax was to Appalachia.

Randolph's approach was to first be accepted as a friend, and when he had won someone's trust, he never betrayed it. He once wrote that "I listened to story-tellers in taverns and village stores, on the courthouse steps, at the mill while our corn was a-grinding, beneath the arbors where backwoods Christians congregate. Several of my best pieces were recorded in a house of mourning, when we sat up all night to keep cats away from the corpse." The latter duty was necessary because of a local superstition that if a cat even sniffed a corpse, horrible things would happen to the survivors.

Randolph wrote many collections of stories and took photographs of many people that a decade after his death in 1980 have been recognized as another important contribution. One of the funniest collections was published after his death. It was raunchy stories that couldn't be included in his books that would appear in schools and public libraries. Modesty prevents me from even giving the name of the book, but it involves that something that little boys—and some men—love to do in the snow.

Like so much of pioneer America, the Ozarks had its share of violence, especially during the years following the Civil War when the country was licking its fresh wounds during the confusing Reconstruction Era. In the Branson area were the Bald Knobbers, a vigilante group that held its meetings on a hilltop with no vegetation so they could see anyone coming. The group was immediately popular, and in 1885 they broke into the Taney County jail and lynched two brothers being held for shooting a storekeeper. They called on drunks to scare them into the way of righteousness, and they beat men who were living in sin with a woman, and they beat known adulterers.

The group remained a force for two to three years, committing some murders and to a large degree controlling Taney County. Eventually the Bald Knobbers faded away as some members went to jail, others were killed, and plain fatigue set in.

The tourist industry was born with Wright's *Shepherd of the Hills* and it has grown steadily over the years. Silver Dollar

City, an Ozarks theme park, became a success, and a local musical group called the Bald Knobbers—of course—built a theater for their performances after the auditorium they used in the city hall became too small. This was the start of the country music explosion in Branson. The Presley family came next and built their own theater, then the Foggy River Boys, then the Plummer family, then the Bob-O-Links.

Boxcar Willie was the first big-name performer; he was followed by the Sons of the Pioneers, Mel Tillis, Ray Stevens, Johnny and June Carter Cash, Andy Williams, and Willie Nelson, among many others. When this book was written, the number was around two dozen.

The best definition of the Branson success came from one singer who said he would much rather the fans come to him at one place rather than having to go on the road throughout most of the year, taking himself to the fans.

The success of Branson has created one of the biggest permanent traffic jams in the Midwest. I drove through in the middle of the week and found myself trapped in traffic that barely moved along. At the first opportunity I made a U-turn, without collecting a fine, and drove to US 65 and north to Springfield.

In the Area

Greater West Plains Area Chamber of Commerce
(West Plains): 417-256-4433

Bull Shoals Lake & White River Area (Theodosia):
417-273-4362

Gainesville Chamber of Commerce (Gainesville):
417- 679-3321

Branson Lakes Area Chamber of Commerce (Branson):
417-334-4136

11 ~

The Gristmill Loop

From Gainsville, in south-central Missouri, drive north on State 5 to State 95. Follow it north to County N and turn north to the Rockbridge resort. Follow County N south to State 181 and turn left (east) to Zanoni. Stay on State 181 to Hodgson Mill. Continue on State 181 to County H, then go south (right) to County PP to the Dawt Mill. Continue on County PP to US 160 near Tecumseh, twenty-six miles west of West Plains.

Highlights: *Four gristmills in various states of repair, one of which is mostly a decoration for a beautiful bed and breakfast and another is the centerpiece of a resort.*

The driving instructions above are as confusing as they sound unless you have a detailed map with all county roads shown. You can probably get a free map from the Chamber of Commerce in West Plains or Gainesville.

Spending a day visiting these mills is a pleasant way to see some of the out-of-the-way places in the Ozarks and to talk to the people who own or operate the mills today. None, by the way, are still in commercial operation and only one still functions at all, but all can be visited.

Those of us who grew up in the Ozarks before World War II have memories of these mills, and it was a lucky day when we could go with our father to the mill with a load of corn or wheat to be ground, because it meant a day without a lot of work, and a chance to hear the machinery creaking and groaning, and to watch the big wheel being turned by the rushing water.

Before I was born, a similar mill stood on Lick Creek only two miles from our farm, but it went out of business. The Dawt Mill was the closest, roughly ten miles away, which was a long trip in a wagon. Can there be any vehicle more miserable than what we called iron-tired wagons? The first wagon we had didn't have a hint of a suspension system, just the wooden wheels with iron or steel hoops. Later my brother and I had the wonderful job of tearing apart a junked Ford Model T our father bought somewhere. The wheels and frame became our first rubber-tired wagon, which was the difference between a yacht and a raft.

Visiting these mills will give you an idea of how isolated many people were in the Ozarks until World War II and beyond.

The Rockbridge gristmill on Spring Creek is probably the oldest of the group. Nobody is quite certain when the first one was built on this site, only that it predated the Civil War. After that mill was built, the town of Rockbridge grew around it, and for a while it was the seat of Ozark County. The little town had a bank, a general store, and a church, along with several homes, but its remote location was its undoing. Gainesville took over while Rockbridge declined to the point that the gristmill was the only thing left.

The town site and mill were in a bad state of decline when Lile and Edith Amyx bought the whole works in 1954 and began restoring the village and mill. It is now a popular resort complex called the Rainbow Trout & Game Ranch. The owners keep Spring Creek stocked with rainbow trout for guests

Hodgson Mill

to catch. Cabins have been built around the general store, which also houses a restaurant, gift shop, and café.

The Zanoni mill was built on Pine Creek about the time of the Civil War, and at one time shared the creek with a water-powered sawmill. The mill was a natural social center; one owner used the upper floor as a dance hall until the mill burned in 1905. Another mill was built on the site, and it continued operating until 1951. Not much is left of the mill today. It is part of a complex on the man-made lake that includes a large colonial home with guest rooms.

The Aid-Hodgson Mill is the best known of the four because it has been used in Salem cigarette commercials, and the late Euell Gibbons used it as a backdrop for his cereal commercials.

Technically it is the Hodgson Mill, but for a long time it was a partnership between the Aid and Hodgson families, and most old-timers call it by its double name. The school-house red building is very picturesque, with old trees framing it and a small waterfall in front that seems to command you to take photographs. The afternoon sun lights the front and the waterfall. Autumn is the best time for photos because of the colors and also because the leaves are so thick in the summer that you can hardly see through them to the mill. The Missouri Department of Tourism says this is the most frequently photographed mill in the state.

The mill was built against a steep hillside and over a spring that produces nearly 29 million gallons of water daily for Bryant River. The mill houses a store and gift shop.

The Dawt Mill (fifty years ago it was already being called the Old Dawt Mill) is on a high bank over the Norfork River, where the river still runs free. The low dam still stands. The mill is the only one that still functions, and it offers demonstrations of milling cornmeal, flour, and feed, as well as black-smithing and other Ozarks crafts. It is a beautiful spot for a picnic, and the store sells food and gifts. A bridge leads down from the mill and across the narrow river for a fine view of the tall mill on the high bluff.

In the Area

Rainbow Trout & Game Ranch (Rockbridge): 417-679-3619

Zanoni Mill Inn (Zanoni): 417-679-4050

Aid-Hodgson Mill (Sycamore): 417-261-2568

Dawt Mill (Tecumseh): 417-284-3540

Index

Other titles in the Country Roads series:

Country Roads of Connecticut and Rhode Island
Country Roads of Florida
Country Roads of Hawaii
Country Roads of Illinois, second edition
Country Roads of Indiana
Country Roads of Kentucky
Country Roads of the Maritimes
Country Roads of Massachusetts
Country Roads of Michigan, second edition
Country Roads of New Jersey
Country Roads of New Hampshire
Country Roads of New York
Country Days in New York City
Country Roads of North Carolina
Country Roads of Ohio
Country Roads of Ontario
Country Roads of Oregon
Country Roads of Pennsylvania
Country Roads of Tennessee
Country Roads of Vermont
Country Roads of Virginia
Country Roads of Washington

All books are $9.95 at bookstores.
Or order directly from the publisher (add $3.00
shipping & handling for direct orders):
Country Roads Press
P.O. Box 286
Castine, Maine 04421
Toll-free phone number: **800-729-9179**